CHEMO PILGRIM

CHEMO PILGRIM

An 18-Week Journey of
Healing and Holiness

CRICKET COOPER

Church Publishing
NEW YORK

Church Publishing
19 East 34th Street
New York, NY 10016
www.churchpublishing.org

Front cover PET scan courtesy of Fletcher Allen Health Center. Thoracic cavity 6/8/2012. Property of the author.

Cover design by Jennifer Kopec, 2Pug Design

Typeset by PerfecType, Nashville, TN

Library of Congress Cataloging-in-Publication Data
Names: Cooper, Cricket, author.
Title: Chemo pilgrim : an 18-week journey of healing and holiness / Cricket
   Cooper.
Description: New York : Church Publishing, 2017.
Identifiers: LCCN 2016041260 (print) | LCCN 2016051944 (ebook) | ISBN
   9780819233134 (pbk.) | ISBN 9780819233141 (ebook)
Subjects: LCSH: Cooper, Cricket. | Lymphomas--Patients--United
   States--Biography. | Lymphomas--Treatment. |
   Lymphomas--Patients--Religious life. | Pilgrims and pilgrimages--United
   States. | Healing--Religious aspects--Christianity.
Classification: LCC BV4910.33 .C665 2017 (print) | LCC BV4910.33 (ebook) |
   DDC 248.8/61969940092 [B] --dc23
LC record available at https://lccn.loc.gov/2016041260

Printed in the United States of America

for Max

"How on earth do you do it? Again and again you say words to me, or pose questions that shine a light into me and make me clear to myself."
—*Narcissus and Goldmund,* by Herman Hesse

CONTENTS

Acknowledgments   ix

Introduction   1

Chemo Round One   33

Weston Priory   43

Chemo Round Two   59

New Skete   71

Chemo Round Three   83

Karma Triyana Dharmachakra   89

Chemo Round Four   101

Zen Mountain Monastery   117

Chemo Round Five   133

Walking the Sacred Path   139

Chemo Round Six   145

Rhinebeck   151

Radiation   157

Epilogue   171

ACKNOWLEDGMENTS

I am deeply grateful for my life, and for the opportunity to tell the story of this journey. A heartfelt thank you to my editor, Nancy Bryan, who believed this was a book several years before it came into being, and for her patience in waiting these four years for it to appear.

For Tom Tuthill, to whom goes the Oscar for Best Supporting Actor. Tom, you were on this journey too, long-distance. Thank you for the days you drove to Burlington and back to do my grocery shopping, renew my prescriptions, or bring the dogs up for a playdate. Thank you from the bottom of my heart.

I owe my life to my medical team. To Emil, Kristen, Paul, Julian, Ruth, and the scores of nurses without whose gentleness, care, compassion, and scientific skill I would not have lived. And to the University of Vermont Medical Center (then Fletcher Allen Health Center), for consistently being a place of compassion and healing on every level.

Particular thanks to Drs. Terryl Kinder and David Bell for generously letting me live in their condo on the Winooski River during the final stages of writing this book. Your gift of quiet, scholarly retreat space inspired and supported me.

I'm grateful to Williams College, for the intense peace and quiet of the Sawyer Library, in whose nooks and crannies I wrote on my days off throughout this spring.

Thank you to my parish of St. Stephen's, Pittsfield, Massachusetts, for the leave time I needed to prepare the final manuscript, and for your encouragement of this project.

A special shout-out to Chris, my spiritual director. I do not know what kind angel shoved me in your direction, but your knowledge of the interplay of body/mind/spirit, your appreciation of meditation, and your own extensive experience in writing and publishing often gave me just the push, encouragement, or belly laugh I most needed, when I most needed it.

For my clergy colleagues, my email Prayer Warriors, and my parishioners and friends in New London, New Hampshire, who were the only people I told about the cancer in the first months, and who prayed, cheered, shook their fists with me at God, and otherwise thoroughly convinced me again about the power of prayer. To my bishops at the time, Gene Robinson and Tom Ely, who were rocks, my New Hampshire clergy peeps (especially Kathleen and Mary—we *are* the champions!), and to the congregation, choir, and staff of The Cathedral Church of St. Paul in Burlington, Vermont, who reminded how very sweet life is. Thank you especially to Mark, Stan, and Diane.

For my family, who all showed up.

My mom and dad, my sister Cat and brother Hap and their families, who appeared in person but also surprised me continually with gifts, treats, and inappropriate humor to keep my mind off my worries. Special gratitude to my sister-in-law Jennifer Cooper, who always asked detailed questions about how I was feeling, and had thoughtful responses and helpful suggestions. My deep affection and respect go to Jennifer's mom, Bobette Lister, whose tenacity fighting non-Hodgkin's lymphoma ten years before I did and participation in clinical trials saved the lives of so many of us who came after.

For my beloved Cellmates, for your immediate response to my diagnosis, and the whirlwind of spinning and knitting that brought friends and strangers together to create the Magic Shawl: Ellen, Joan, Deb, Jan, Erica, KarenJ, Joc, KarenG, Lisa, Peggy. Over and over again, you always know just the right thing to say, do, or knit. Your messages, gifts, and constant affection got me through the worst times.

For the religious communities of Weston Priory, New Skete, Zen Mountain Monastery, Karma Triyana Dharmachakra, and Gampo Abbey. A deep bow to you all, in gratitude for your unquestioning welcome for all people. May you know that your teachings and friendship change lives.

I am grateful to Megan Kowalewski, whose video "Stronger" on YouTube became an anthem and fight song for me and for many thousands of others. What a gift, Megan!

A standing ovation to my friends who were fighting their own cancers while I fought mine. For Bryan, Chris, Cheryl, and Margaret. We're still here, friends. Stay strong.

Finally, much love to the dear ones I lost while on my journey.

For Jay, who passed away two weeks before my diagnosis. Thank you for giving me that push on May 20.

For my Dad, who passed away while I was still on my journey..

For Dexter, who passed away just as I was starting my final treatment. Your delight in my life and my adventures, while quietly fighting your own leukemia, gave me the biggest laughs and happiest tears in my journey. Order champagne, and save me a seat on the banquette up there, OK?

AMDG

INTRODUCTION

Midway upon the journey of our life
I found myself within a forest dark,
For the straightforward pathway had been lost.
Ah me!
　—Canto 1, *The Inferno*, Dante Alighieri (tr. H. W. Longfellow)

Every now and then, do you just "wake up" in a moment, and look around and think, "Really? *This* is my life?" To paraphrase the old Talking Heads song, suddenly the light shifts or our vision sharpens and everything looks odd, and we think that this is not our beautiful house, not our beautiful life.

I "woke up" one summer morning in July 2012 in the cool basement of a Zen Buddhist monastery, seated on a toilet seat with a syringe in my hand.

At 6:55 am I'd already been awake for two hours, seated in the zendo in meditation and at the morning Buddhist worship service. Now I had slipped away from breakfast into the basement to grab one of my prepackaged Neupogen shots out of the employee refrigerator and casually strolled to the bathroom to shoot up. What was it about walking around with a syringe that made me feel furtive and embarrassed, every single time?

The Neupogen was to help me rebuild white blood cells following my recent dose of chemotherapy. I was in the bathroom of a Zen monastery . . . why? Because the only way I could visualize this journey—cancer and chemo and the rest of my messy life—was by reimagining it, reframing it.

Like Dante, I was indeed "midway on the journey of life," three days before my fifty-first birthday. I did not want to have cancer. I did not want to do chemo. But I *could* imagine myself on a pilgrimage, a spiritual journey filled with danger, and hope and blessing and surprise. A journey, I dare say, that has a Beginning . . . and an End.

And so, the week I was diagnosed with non-Hodgkin's lymphoma, my brain—grasping at a way to move through those upcoming months of treatment—reframed "cancer" and "chemo" and the challenges to come as a spiritual pilgrimage.

I have always longed to go on pilgrimage. Suddenly, I did not have to travel to Mecca, or Jerusalem, or Santiago de Compostela. All I had to do was pull on my shoes and step out into my own life.

My life was already in flux. My fiftieth birthday and my twenty-second ordination anniversary had been a pivot point for me. Twenty-two years of parish work had me longing for the refreshment of something intellectually clear and clean, like science. I come from a family of women scientists, and yet had never allowed myself to wander far from language, theology, and the arts. As my fiftieth birthday had approached and other friends of mine worked on doctorates in ministry or congregational development, I found myself seeking refreshment from the constant gray areas of ministry by taking online classes in speech pathology and neuroscience, disciplines I had loved in college.

The month of my fiftieth birthday, I wrenched myself from a parish and community I deeply cared for in New Hampshire, packed up the car, kissed my husband and the dogs goodbye, and drove to the University of Vermont to work on a master's degree in communication disorders. My husband, Tom, would remain in New Hampshire with his job, our house, and our three dogs for the duration of my studies.

My academic advisor had jokingly welcomed us to the program by saying that we had many choices we could make in order to succeed in the program, like deciding what to give up: eating, sleeping, or using the bathroom. His teasing good humor turned into my reality, as I plunged into the course of study with my whole being. The hobbies and distractions I'd imagined Burlington, Vermont, would offer were a distant memory within days. Tropical Storm Irene slammed into the state our first week of classes, but I was so anemic already that the Red Cross wouldn't accept my blood, though they were desperate for donations. Still studying many nights at 2:00 am, I would reach for a granola bar or a bowl of cereal, holding the food above my books as I blinked back the weariness and memorized the cranial nerves or the wavy patterns of hearing loss. I was madly in love with the work, even as I struggled to embrace an entirely new discipline. Fighting to keep my head above water, I crashed my way through to the end of the school year. A week and a half after finals, everything changed.

It was Jay who saved my life.

Jay and I were friends and housemates in college. He and I had lived a mindful life together, long before that term became popular, sharing an apartment our senior year. Night after night, we would sit down to the dinner we had cooked, and spend two or three minutes in silence, simply looking at and appreciating the meal. Only when we both had appreciated our dinner with our eyes and our noses would one of us finally pick up fork or spoon, and we would dig into that night's creation. All these years later, Jay lived near me in Vermont, so we were able to grab lunch and check in from time to time. We had both graduated from Northwestern University's creative writing department, and he continued to write poetry and had published a book called *Living with Chickens*. I also wrote regularly, but more in my capacity as an Episcopal parish priest, writing sermons, short news-letter articles, and the occasional poem. Now that I was in graduate school, I was back to writing papers, and I dearly missed letting the right side of my brain do some writing, too.

Earlier that year, we had been talking seriously about getting together for more formal writing and critique time, but finding just the right day to meet up was tricky as Jay was battling an exception-ally aggressive strain of prostate cancer. The year before, he had trav-eled twice to Denmark for treatments not available in this country. In March of 2012, Jay reflected in an email,

> I got into a pretty bad place with the cancer last fall, everyone but me thought I was going to die before Christmas. . . . I started chemotherapy at the beginning of December and it has made an incredible difference. I look much more normal.

I replied,

> I also would love to have some time to talk to you about the cancer thing. And [its] mind-body impact, connection. A friend has just found out she has a really nasty breast cancer. I'm a little freaked . . . but hearing about things not only from your per-spective, but from inside the body being treated . . . that would be important learning for me.

It is downright eerie for me to revisit this conversation from March, knowing my cancer would be discovered in May; at the time I wrote this email my "important learning" was already growing inside of me.

Jay and I swapped emails a few more times around Easter, but weren't able to connect our schedules. He had been feeling poorly that week anyway, so I gave him a few weeks to build his strength back up, as had been the pattern.

On May 19, I gathered with hundreds of colleagues and friends in Concord, New Hampshire, for the election of a new bishop. Though I was away in graduate school in Vermont, I was still able to cast a ballot for the next bishop of New Hampshire. As I grabbed a quick cup of coffee before the morning began, I bumped into a colleague who was also the priest at the church where Jay had been going. I mentioned Jay's name cheerfully and my friend's face froze. I knew exactly what that meant.

"Oh my God, no. Please, please tell me he's OK?"

My friend shook his head. "Oh, Cricket. His funeral was last week."

It was like being handed a hundred stones when you are wearing a dress without pockets; I had absolutely nowhere to put that information. Jay was dead? Jay? Dead?

In the very next moment, I had to turn and walk into the church where I would see dozens of dear friends for the first time since I'd moved to Vermont the year before. I took this impossible news, tucked it somewhere deep down inside of me, took a breath, and walked into the space where my friends were gathering.

A few surreal hours later, I climbed into my car for the three-hour drive home and started to cry, even before I turned the car on. I cried the entire trip home. Shocked. Wounded. When I reached my apartment, the crying escalated. I howled in hurt that we had missed seeing each other in that month or two because, at fifty years old, death wasn't in our equation. The recent emails about poetry and chicken butchering had been in our usual chatty tone. I couldn't believe he was gone, and that I'd even missed a chance to honor him at his funeral.

It was as hard a night as I'd ever had. Late in the evening, I showered and pulled the shreds of my heart together. In the morning I would be celebrating the 8:00 am service at the cathedral in Burlington, so I needed to grab a little sleep. I set the alarm for Too Early, lay my weary, sore face on my pillow, and conked out.

In the morning, I actually felt much better. Surprised, I took another shower, and went to the cathedral. The simple service was over in less than an hour, and I was back in the car, contemplating where to enjoy Sunday brunch.

Except something was not right. I felt an odd, slight twinge in the right half of my chest. It didn't seem like a heart-related thing. My pulse felt natural and my breathing seemed normal. But still, there it was again. Not much, but more than nothing. I thought through the day before. Had I done anything that would have pulled a muscle in my chest? I had vigorously hugged probably one hundred and fifty people, being reunited with so many friends and colleagues in New Hampshire. Then I had cried for five or six hours. It seemed to me that either of these things might have caused the subtle, sore twinge I was feeling. It was probably nothing. Nevertheless, I just didn't feel like going to brunch. I pulled over and settled into the front window seat of a coffee shop with a massive mug of dark roast coffee and waited for the twinge to pass.

Two hours later, I was still there. I couldn't decide what to do next. I had recently begun a mindfulness meditation practice, and so I closed my eyes and let my imagination scan through my body, let it be curious about what was going on.

What I saw was Jay, standing in front of me.

The kind of friend who encourages and even goads you, Jay was never shy about telling me what was on his mind. There, silhouetted by the bright sunlight, I could see him clearly, leaning toward me. "Cricky," he was saying, "I'm OK now. I'm healed. Now it's about you. You need to get this checked." In my mind's eye, he was tapping his long forefinger on the sore spot just below my collarbone. "Cricky," he kept insisting, "Get. This. Checked." I got into the car that minute, and drove to the emergency room of the local hospital.

It was a blessedly slow afternoon at Fletcher Allen Health Center. The pleasant young ER doctor and I chatted happily as he ran the requisite electrocardiogram (EKG), blood pressure, and other medical scans on me. One test after another came up perfectly normal, so I was more certain that this was probably just a pulled muscle. I was starting to shuffle back into my shoes when he glanced back into the cubicle. "Hey, would you mind just going for an x-ray? I can't imagine there's anything to see, but that's the only thing I haven't done. There's no wait, I could get you right in."

I shrugged. Why not? I was here anyway, and would get slammed with that hundred-dollar student health fee for this Sunday visit in any event. May as well walk down to x-ray.

Twenty minutes later, as I was finally pulling my socks and shoes back on in my emergency room cubicle, the curtain was drawn aside and my friendly young doctor said, "Hey! Come look at this with me, OK?" I stepped over to his screen, and saw all of the organ blobs one sees in an x-ray. "This," he said, tapping at a large area, "this is your heart here. But this?" He tapped another large blob. "Do you have any idea what this might be? It shouldn't be there." He looked at me quizzically.

My year in speech pathology hadn't prepared me for a pop quiz about the organs of the chest. "No idea. None at all," I said.

The doctor's face went still, and I was tucked back into the cubicle while he made a rapid series of hushed calls. The words that drifted over my curtain were not reassuring. "No, sir, I have no idea. . . . Really large, sir. The same size as her heart. . . . I don't think she should leave. Should I admit her?"

Now I felt like I was having a heart attack. My breathing was ragged, and my heart was in my throat. What on earth was going on?

After a very long silence, the young doctor came back in, only now his cheerful, chatty manner had changed to a more detached, professional one. "We're going to bring you in tomorrow to get that checked. May need a CT scan, or a biopsy. I'll have them call you with the next available appointment time, OK? Will you be at this number the rest of the day?" He showed me my intake form with my cell phone number on it. I nodded and thanked him, and was turning away, but not before I saw the flash of fear in his eyes.

The unidentified mass was discovered in my chest on May 20, and I hoped (the way you do, when you don't quite understand the big picture) that this wouldn't disturb my plans for June. Two weeks later, I was supposed to fly to Washington, DC, for a friend's retirement ceremony from the Navy, then to Baltimore to attend my niece's high school graduation, and then settle into an uneventful summer, catching my breath after an overwhelming year of graduate school.

Though I didn't yet know the scope of the danger I was in, decades of serving as a parish priest had left me fascinated by medical puzzles. Here's some advice: If you ever find yourself in this situation, stay off the internet.

I admit I am nobody to tell anyone to stay off the internet. I know that the first, most natural thing to do these days is to take the sketchy information you may have about an illness (your own or someone else's), and run to the internet to google whatever you know. One family member of mine inexplicably sat at his desk for an hour reading up on symptoms of a heart attack *while having chest pains*. My mass was tentatively identified as a "probably benign, thymic neoplasm." That sounds like something, doesn't it? But when I ran to the internet, mostly all I learned was that it was a growth of unknown origin or makeup that was now residing near my thymus gland. Not super helpful.

And yet, would it have helped me if this dense article in the *Journal of Thoracic Disease* had been published by then? Here, the abstract helpfully offers this concise description:

> Thymic neoplasms constitute a broad category of rare lesions with a wide spectrum of pathologic characteristics and clinical presentations which therefore require a high index of suspicion to diagnose. The natural history of the disease is seldom predictable, anywhere from an indolent to an aggressively malignant course. Although the classification and staging of these lesions are complex and controversial, complete radical surgical

resection remains the gold standard of therapy. Radiation and chemotherapy are important elements of the multimodality approach to treating these patients. . . .[1]

What words jump out at me as I read this? *Rare. Suspicion. Seldom predictable. Aggressively malignant. Complex. Controversial. Radical surgical resection.*

Now magnify the impact of these words by the fact that my web search brought up 119,000 results, and these words are all found *in just* the first paragraph of the first article *alone*. Oh. My. God.

The next day, the hospital called to say it would be eight days until there was an opening in the schedule for a CT-guided needle biopsy. An appointment was made, and I hung up the phone, incredulous. Eight days? Eight days of walking around, feeling as if I'd swallowed a land mine? Were they joking?

Eight days to wait, knowing there was a fist-sized, unidentified mass leaning against my lung. I was told that they wanted to move fast because if it grew appreciably more, it could lean into the wrong vein and cut off the blood supply to my heart. Not good.

Of course, I immediately went online to check out what the thing might be. I emailed my parents and siblings at 7:00 on Monday morning, and in minutes my brother Hap fired back a David Letterman–esque "Top 10 Things Your Unidentified Thoracic Mass Might Be . . ."

10. The ham sandwich you had yesterday "went down the wrong way"
 9. A thumbprint from the ER nurse interrupted from eating her s'more
 8. Way-ectopic pregnancy

---

1. Omar M. Rashid, Anthony D. Cassano, and Kazuaki Takabe, "Thymic Neoplasm: A Rare Disease With a Complex Clinical Presentation," *Journal of Thoracic Disease* 5, no. 2 (April 2013), http://jtd.amegroups.com/article/view/914/html.

7. Your kidney had to go to the bathroom and went down the wrong hall

6. A sign that you're getting a new job—arming you for stronger empathy

5. An alien about to burst through your chest and threaten the free world (you had to see the movie)

4. Really nothing—but you should give me the family silver now as a precaution

3. Your torn meniscus found a place to have a family

2. Reabsorbed twin

1. Muscle tissue built from years of making the sign of the cross

Our family humor can be seriously off-base, and we can wield it as a shield against feeling, as a distraction, as a desperate raft of incongruity when something upsetting is unfolding. But I have to say, it was a comfort to me in that week to have other people making fun of "Chester" (what the mass was immediately nicknamed), and reframing the news and fear as absurd.

I wrote to everyone—friends, colleagues, family members. I asked for prayers, and also assured people that I had no signs of any cancer or other alarming disease in my bloodstream or on the x-rays. Lymphoma was usually confirmed by an elevated lactate dehydrogenase (LDH) level in the blood, but my levels were well within normal range. I took a lot of comfort in these small signs. At the same time, I sent the x-ray off to a family friend who was a doctor, just to see what other thoughts a professional might have. Dan's calm reply settled me in those waiting days.

The world was swirling. One minute laughing, one minute anxious, one minute feeling calm and centered, the next minute feeling surreal, like this was a strange dream and I'd wake up any minute. At night, I'd lie in bed, breathing and trying to "feel" the mass in my chest. Even the twinge that had called my attention to it in the first place had gone away while I was still in the ER that day. I felt nothing out of the ordinary. When the fear began to rise up into my throat, I would place my hands over the spot where I had seen the frighteningly large mass beside my heart, and I would talk to it, as if it were a scared child or animal. Soothingly, I would talk late into the night, welcoming it to my chest. There was no sense *not* welcoming it—it was there. And telling it to go away seemed counterintuitive. If we were going to be spending time together, I wanted us to be on the same team. "Ah, hello in there. How are you doing? Where did you come from?" Pressing my hands against the area, I would croon, "Can you feel this? I'm sending healing light into you. Feel the warmth? Feel the light. It's not good for you to be hiding in there in the darkness. Welcome. I know you're there. Peace to you, peace."

C. S. Lewis, when asked if prayer changed anything, said that he didn't know for sure, but prayer changed him and that was enough. Singing, praying, visualizing the mass helped me in ways I can barely put into words. Most important for me, however, was not to think of it as "Me vs. It," not to think of it as an evil intruder. It was honestly a part of me, and so I wanted to calm myself, to imagine that, like a liver or kidney, this mass was just living peaceably in my chest. . . .

I wrote to a good friend that week, a retired gerontologist who'd spent his working years in the hospital, and I told him about Chester. His response, which I read while sitting in a coffee shop, was fast and firm:

> I have something similar in my groin (not *there*!). I call it Oscar. I think it is important to put a real name to these things that become attached to us—you know, befriend them. Oscar is just there. We have occasional conversations. It is nice that we can just pick-up where we left off—just like a friend.
>
> I know that Oscar would like to meet your new friend (now this is sounding really weird). Hell, when can we get together?

I almost snorted five dollars' worth of dark roast right out of my nose onto the computer screen. His words, the perfect friendly tone just when I needed them, doubled me over until I could see folks at the nearby tables seeming to say with their expressions, "Whoa, a little too much caffeine over there?"

The invitation for Oscar to meet Chester was especially calming. Suddenly I wasn't alone with this strange thing; other people actually had them too, and just lived life with secret neoplasms hidden away in their bodies. We set a time to have dinner and I could feel my shoulders release their tension. "You've got this," I thought. With friends and loved ones rallying . . . you *have* this.

I had the CT-guided biopsy the Tuesday after Memorial Day. I was told that I would be placed in the CT machine, which would guide a needle into my chest, through my chest wall, and into the mass, selectively removing a sample for testing. Depending on the size and homogenous aspect of the mass, they might do this once or multiple times. I would be sedated all the while.

As someone blissfully unaware of hospital procedures, I couldn't make up my mind if this was something to be nervous about. It sounded ghastly, but I also felt pretty certain that it was a benign mass, and so this test would give me what I was assuming would be good news. At the time, my biggest concern was how they'd remove Chester after the biopsy.

My friend and neighbor, Ann, picked me up early in the morning, since I wouldn't be able to drive home after the procedure. Insightful and unflappable, she greeted me as I opened the car door, asking, "Are you nervous?" Deep inside me there was a grabbing feeling, and I knew I had two choices: to make a quick reply or completely unravel. I chose the former. "Nope—I'm good to go," I said, and she proceeded to chatter kindly during the drive to keep me distracted.

I was led into the procedure room, which seemed large and scary. Machinery was everywhere, and the bed in the middle of it all looked small and hard. Feeling like a very expensive cut of steak, I allowed the prep team to lay me out, position this bit or that bit of my body, prop me all around with foam blocks, strap me firmly in place with wide bands of Velcro (changing positions while having a long needle stuck through my chest seemed like a serious "no-no"), start an IV line, pull up the massive scanning machinery, and otherwise go about their work in a calm, orderly fashion.

While preparing for surgery or a surgical procedure, there aren't a lot of ways that a medical team can really spend time on pastoral care. Their job is to get a procedure done efficiently and accurately. But almost every medical professional I've known in the past thirty years has also understood that, at the center of all these procedures, there is a human being, and that gentleness and concern for the patient's experience is a huge unwritten part of the work. That's why, in the middle of being positioned and prodded, and tucked and undraped, and marked and measured, a nurse kindly asked if I would like a warm blanket.

What a simple thing. They have stacks and stacks of these in a warmer close at hand. I don't know what part of my brain responded to this small act of kindness and comfort, but being wrapped up by another person in a warm blanket took me back, somatically, to the preverbal time of infanthood. I don't know if the clinically warmed blanket existed as such in 1961, when I was born, and I don't know if I was ever wrapped in one, but the power of the lightly warmed blanket and the feeling of gentle hands tucking the edges around my body was transformational. I'm a caregiver, and it is often hard for me to accept gestures of kindness or comfort from others. My wiring doesn't quite know how to receive the very signals that I am so used to giving to others. The warm blanket cut through words and automatic responses, cut through my own professionalism and need to be the caregiver. Suddenly, I was infinitely tiny and precious, and being swaddled with a kind of meticulous affection that touched me to my very core.

All things being ready, the doctor performing the procedure told me he was about to start the IV, and that I would quickly become sleepy. This is always a great moment. The anxiety of waiting for this day, and the stress of coming in and getting prepped is all finished. With the pull of the medication, you can lie back and let the good people do their work. I smiled at the technicians and nurses all around the table and wished them well with the procedure. Then the gal with the sedation drugs said, "OK, off you go," and that was that.

A very gentle man's voice was my next sensation. "Thanks for the concert," he murmured to me, as I blinked in the bright light a few times.

"Gah. . . Whaa?" I may or may not have said aloud.

"You've been singing for an hour—it was great. I've never had a sedated patient sing to me. Thanks." He smiled at me, curiously, and my still-fogged brain wondered when they would just hurry up and start the procedure. But, of course, they were finished and tidying up.

I was shifted to another table and unceremoniously transferred to a recovery room to sleep off the drugs. Behind me, as I was wheeled away on my gurney, I had the sense of all of the team readying the room to do the entire procedure over again, with the next patient. I felt an infinite tenderness for these people, who spent all day, every day, positioning one nervous human body after another, starting IVs and watching the person drift away, so the team could extract from deep within some key to the mystery that dwelt within each one of us. For a time, they had been my team, and now they would shift gears and become someone else's.

These are the days I can't bear to revisit. If I thought I had become progressively more and more insane *before* the biopsy, then afterward, as I was waiting for the results, I got even worse. On the outside, a person can get dressed, walk around, smile, and function, while on the inside everything feels like it's falling apart. My inner life felt like a bad community theatre dress rehearsal of *Les Miserables*. Wailing. People in rags. Death. Loss. Lots of overacting.

That week before the biopsy results came back, I did everything I could to distract myself. I went on the tour at Ben and Jerry's. I renewed my driver's license. I had lunch with friends, and reassured them that this would be nothing. I went to Tai Chi, where my class-mates surrounded me with healing light and energy. I even wrote a sonnet to my unidentified mass, trying to make peace with it.

The next weekend, I was signed up to attend a retreat on cre-ation theology with Matthew Fox. Once a Catholic priest and now an Episcopal priest, Matt is a true modern visionary who writes about the goodness of creation and the holiness of our human lives and bodies.[2]

I knew I would get my diagnosis on Friday, and so it seemed perfect to take that news with me into a weekend of wildly inclusive theology, conversations about care for creation, and care for ourselves and bodies. I knew I would be facing something serious, probably a chest surgery, and where better to process the information than the Episcopal retreat center, called Adelynrood, in the midst of gentle, kindly people?

Except the diagnosis was delayed. Having to wait from Friday to Monday for some things would not be a big deal, but honestly, when I heard that the short holiday week meant they were one day off in getting tests through the lab, I went a *little* crazy. I called the student health office, hoping they had the information, but they didn't have a chance to meet with me until Monday. I kept calling throughout the afternoon, hoping to get someone on the phone who would indis-creetly open my file and blurt out the answer. No luck.

Getting nowhere with them, I *might* have called the hospital lab, possibly allowing them to believe I was calling from UVM student health. I'm not saying I did, but I can imagine a world in which that might have happened. . . . Nope. The results were not in, not anywhere.

So off to Matt Fox I went, for a wonderful, inspirational weekend filled with hope for the future. I swallowed down the rising fear and

---

2. A recently revised volume of his is titled *Sins of the Spirit, Blessings of the Flesh*. People who have suffered as the Church has driven a wedge between being human and being whole have been deeply moved and healed by Matt's work.

anxiety and reminded myself to breathe. Reminded myself to do my meditation. Reminded myself to enjoy the day I had. It was still a perfect weekend, and Monday rolled around eventually as I'd known it would.

I was working hard to maintain a calm exterior as I waited for my doctor at student health, tapping my fingers on the chair in a manner I hoped looked more musical than neurotic. He came into the office, kind of chipper. "How are you?" he asked.

I wanted to leap into the air and shriek, "Seriously? Am I here for chit-chat?"

Biting my tongue, my lips, the inside of my cheeks, I managed a smile. "So far, so good," I replied.

He sat down and said, in a strangely casual way, "Well, we're dealing with a cancer here . . . it's diffuse large B-cell lymphoma," and he kept talking. Meanwhile, my brain derailed from the track and started to spin. I remember working to keep my face absolutely still, maintaining eye contact, nodding and leaning forward to absorb words that were just running through my head without being processed.

My very first thought: He's going to be embarrassed when he realizes these are someone else's results, and someone has mixed up the files.[3]

My second thought: Will I still get to make the pilgrimage I'd been planning this summer?

By now, my doctor was generously sharing the fact that he was also a cancer-survivor. He was rattling on about tests and staging. My eyes noticed that he seemed optimistic, but nothing else was registering in my brain. It was as if the inside of my head had been coated in Teflon and thoughts simply slipped around without getting any traction.

---

3. Having spoken with friends who have received a cancer diagnosis about the moment of their diagnoses, many of them admitted that their very first thought was also complete denial.

As I reread my emails from June 2012, in which I tell family and friends about the mass and then about the biopsy results, I am struck by my overwhelmingly calm voice. I know I was afraid that if other people reacted in an anxious, frightened way, that alone would scare me. Over and over again, I say, "This is at a very early stage, and is a type they expect will react quickly and completely to chemo." I talk about the chemo like it's a course of penicillin—no more scary or debilitating than that.

I consciously put the information out in a low-key fashion, so as to sound in control, of myself and my emotions, as well as of the cancer and its outcome. I wanted to convince others that this would have an easy cure, but of course I needed to convince myself.

Here is the practice that made all the difference to me. I had been working all that spring with Max, my therapist, on non-labeling and mindfulness. What if I could simply live in each moment without hanging on to the past or imagining the future? It was one thing to apply this mindfulness work to my graduate school schedule or my work as a priest. It was an entirely new ballgame to apply this way of living to a cancer diagnosis. It was also the perfect path to be on at that very moment.

I was especially drawn to this Buddhist practice of non-labeling. We move through our lives constantly judging events, people, items on our to-do list. Everything we see, or think, or encounter gets a little mental label: Good or Bad, Enjoyable or Annoying, Pleasant or Unpleasant.

Then, without realizing what we've done, we treat those items not as they simply are, but rather we react to and experience things *according to the label* we've put on them. In effect, we choose in advance what will bring us joy or what will annoy us, based on past events or current assumptions, before those people or events even come into our day. No wonder some days we drag ourselves out of bed without enthusiasm. If we've already judged everything on our to-do list, and there are more "bad" labels than "good," then we've already labeled the whole day. "It's going to be a hard day, or a long day, or a bad day." If we feel like that at 6:00 am, it's nearly impossible to shake that label, and we *do*, in fact, have a hard, long, or bad day; we have programmed ourselves to experience the day according to the labels we've attached to it.

If you're not used to this way of thinking, it can sound disingenuous. "Cricket, get real. The day is full of unpleasant things. Of course it'll be a bad day." All I am saying is there is another way to frame it. It is possible—I know because I learned how—to unhook our minds from the Velcro of those labels, and suddenly we are free to notice the bird singing on our way to the car, or the softness of that alpaca sweater, or the joy of that first cup of coffee. When your boss greets you in the hall, you don't have to feel dread or anger, but instead you can unhook from judgment and just say "Good morning." You are not ignoring the fact that you may have strong feelings about things, but you are allowing yourself to live in the moment that is—not in a past moment when things were unhappy, or in a future moment when things will be different, but in the very moment of *now*. The only moment, in fact, that actually exists.[4]

This concept of non-labeling was a game changer when my mass was discovered and my cancer diagnosed. It wasn't easy, but with every scrap of information, every invasive test, every needle-stick, every step, I worked hard at saying, "OK, this is just information. It is not good or bad—it is just information." When I forgot and wandered into the future—for example, when I tried to cancel my therapy appointment scheduled for the day after I started chemo because I was certain I would be too sick to come in—Max would remind me patiently, "Let's wait till next Tuesday and just see how you feel that day."

It sounds unbalanced to say that receiving a diagnosis of cancer is neither a good nor bad thing—it smacks of denial, or idiocy, or

---

4. I later heard this practice referred to as "licking the blade of nowness."

emotional untruth. But this was in fact the practice that saved me. Out of the blue, people appeared in my path who would reinforce this way of moving through life with curiosity instead of fear, turning these months of treatment into a time of exploration and openness. If I had labeled those months as "Cancer Treatment: A Bad Thing," I would, I think, have curled up in my tiny apartment and shut down possibilities. By imagining that I was being given a gift of openness, a series of months when I would be neither working nor going to graduate school, but rather a period of "time out of time," in which I could follow a spiritual path that would include chemo but not be wholly *defined* by that. . . . this is where all the doors and windows opened up, and I saw that my perspective could shape the time ahead, and not be a victim of it.

A few weeks earlier, I had been toying with the idea of a summer road trip, a pilgrimage to Gampo Abbey, a Buddhist monastery on the far tip of Cape Breton, Nova Scotia. Much of what I had been learning about moving more gently through life came from the writings and audios of Pema Chödrön, a wise and irreverent nun who lived there. Now, it was clear that that road trip was out of the question, and yet I could still make other choices, choose another pilgrimage. Perhaps I could go on a chemo pilgrimage.

At student health they told me to go home and wait. "You'll get a call from the hospital in a few hours to set up your appointments."

I went back to my apartment, but I couldn't sit down. Words were crashing around in my head in a strange, numb way, like a hailstorm of marshmallows. *Cancer. Chemo. Oncologist. Staging.* These words belonged to other people, to those I've ministered to and sat with. They were not *my* words. I did not want them. Finally, I couldn't pace any more. I have always been very proactive about my health. "I'm not sitting here waiting," I told myself. "I'm going over there."

Fourteen minutes later, I walked confidently into the cancer center at the hospital, like it had been waiting for me all my life. I strode in all smiles, hand extended, full-on eye contact. I approached the oncology desk, beaming like I was accepting an Oscar.

"Hi, I'm newly diagnosed, and am supposed to be getting in touch with Nina. Is she around?" Nina was one of the oncology department's social workers, and my first contact with the department. She was someone to walk me through these first steps, and—I think—probably grade me on the "what can we offer to help this person?" scale. The nonplussed gal at the desk made me repeat my spiel again. "Um . . . name and birthdate, please?" She tapped around on her computer a bit, glancing nervously up at my smiling, confident, healthy-looking face. "Um, let me try this another way . . . when was your diagnosis?" I looked down at my watch and said, "About an hour and a half ago." She blanched, got up, and backed through a door behind her.

I imagine being a social worker for newly diagnosed cancer patients is demanding work. Nina was the first person who would officially meet me as a cancer patient. I was nervous. Would she like me? A different woman came through the door behind the desk and smiled at me. "Nina is just finishing up with a patient. If you will take a seat, she'll be right out."

But I still couldn't sit. I wandered the waiting room, giving wide berth to the display of scarves and turbans and photos of smiling women wearing wigs. *It's the first week of June, and in three days I will be fifty-one. People die at my age. Oh God.*

A few minutes later, Nina came through an invisible door in the wall. Part of the wall simply opened, and there she was. I was the only person in the waiting area.

"Charlotte?" she asked me, smiling gently. I took a deep breath. "Actually, folks call me Cricket, but yes, that's me."

And then we were off.

I met my oncologist at the end of that week. I'd had a series of tests every day to stage the cancer; I was so nervous I was almost sick to my stomach. The doctor was slipping me in at the end of the day, at the end of the week, and chemo was possibly slated for Monday. I was pacing in the exam room like a tiger, and when I'm nervous, I sing. This is how it happened that, alone in the exam room, I was lustily singing "Shall We Dance?" from *The King and I* as I stood in a corner reading a poster about pulmonary embolisms. At one point in the song, as I was nearing the climax of the verse, I swirled around, singing about a new romance, and there, frozen in the half-open doorway, tall and pale and amused, was a stranger—obviously my new doctor. I stopped the song in mid-crescendo, and looked embarrassed, but he laughed and said, "No, no, don't stop on my account!"

As he came in, both of us laughing, I extended my hand. "Hi, I'm Cricket Cooper. Thank you for seeing me today—"

"Gianni Ancilotto," he said. "Forgive me for laughing, but most of my patients aren't singing when I meet them. Please, sit down and tell me what's been going on."

Gianni carefully rolled out the findings of the PET and the other information, and then asked me about any symptoms I might have. I had had a cough, but had assumed it was a lingering thing from a cold I'd just had. What about strange rashes? Night sweats? Anything? I laughed and said, "Night sweats? Hello—I'm a woman in her fifties!" He laughed too, and added, "No—the kind I mean would leave you so soaked, you'd have to get up several times a night and change your pajamas and your sheets?" OMG—the idea of that sobered me quickly. "No, no—nothing like that. Dear God, how frightening that must be."

What we discovered was that I didn't seem to have any accompanying issues, all good signs for staging the cancer. I shook his hand and said, "OK, Gianni, I'm on your team. You just let me know what is mine to do, and I've got it."

He smiled. "Just keep on singing, and you'll be fine."

Throughout my career, I had been with countless people when their doctors told them they had cancer. I had seen everyone turn to the person, offering some solace or strength. Still I was not prepared, the week I was diagnosed with cancer, as I watched the world pivot around me, and found myself suddenly in the center of a circle of care, maybe for the first time in my life. It was mind-boggling. Suddenly, my health and well-being was a priority for dozens of strangers.

Nurses, social workers, doctors, wig makers, dieticians, psychologists, body work professionals, fitness gurus, massage therapists, beauty consultants—suddenly they were all asking me, "What do you need? How can I help?"

This sudden waking up into my own life, and finding myself surrounded by support, did not teach me that having cancer was a great thing, but it did teach me that there are circles of support around us wherever we find ourselves. We just have to open our eyes and look around. It also taught me that relying on others is not a sign of weakness—it's a sign of being human.

I don't go looking for support. I grew up in a family where being self-sufficient was an expectation. For the most part, this was empowering. Mom taught us to think through the situation we were in and come up with a solution. Nevertheless, what I did not learn was how to rely on others. Ever. For anything.

Cancer immediately connected me to strangers, family members, and friends in intensely new ways. Suddenly, my family was everywhere—online, on the phone, showing up at the airport in three hours. Countless friends rallied and sent support within minutes of hearing my news. They were *everywhere*. One of my dearest friends, who was battling breast cancer when I was diagnosed, was having a similar experience; we plotted to run away to an island where we could just share our stories and compare notes.

I realized that I had a terrific national network of friends to lean into. The very next week, I was supposed to go to a mini-reunion of the Virtual Cellmates. We were a gaggle of women scientists, an admiral, a doctor, church and state employees, designers and artists who lived all over the country. We met in 2009 at the Sock Summit, a global gathering of sock knitters in Portland, Oregon.[5] When, after a week, Ellen and Joan and Deb and I laughingly realized that we had become too good a group of friends to disperse forever back to our homes in Washington state, Minneapolis/St. Paul, and New Hampshire, we formed the Cellmates, discovering that via the internet we could stay together, knitting and gabbing long after the summit had ended. As time passed, more friends were pulled into the circle, and our Cell grew bigger.

The reunion centered on Jan's retirement from the Navy. She had secretly asked me to offer a prayer at the ceremony, so I was excited and eager not to let her down. However, as the news of the mass in my chest became more worrisome, I had to bow out of the trip to Washington, DC, so that it could be staged and identified, and a treatment plan designed. Crushed to miss the chance to see them all, I filled them in about the mass and the diagnosis.

Unbeknownst to me, Jan's retirement weekend became the opportunity for my friends to create a shawl for me to wear during my chemo treatments. Secretly, some donated their own handspun or hand-dyed yarns, another designed a pattern, another chose beads and bits of sea glass to adorn the corners. Photos I would see later of Jan's retirement weekend showed the shawl ever present in the background of the event, on a lap in the car on the way to the Pentagon, on a different lap during the ceremony itself. Designed so more than one person could knit it at the same time, the shawl appears in its various growth stages in the center of groups of my friends, and even some total strangers who were put to work on it. That weekend, incredible love and prayers for healing were knit literally into the fabric of this

_____

5. As a parishioner of mine said, when I tried to explain where I was heading on my vacation, "Hmph. That sounds like a tremendous waste of time and energy." Well, yes, I suppose if you aren't passionate about sock knitting, it certainly could seem that way.

gift, and within a few weeks I received it in the mail, wrapping it around me with tears and wonder and delight.

Being wrapped in the love of friends and family was an unlooked-for blessing, but the instant connection I felt to strangers was an even bigger surprise. For example, when I started wearing my wig, I became aware of how many *other* people were wearing wigs. In line at the grocery store, I'd see three other people wearing wigs, and wonder why. Fellow cancer patients? Religious regulations? Thinning hair issues?

Even now, three years after my treatments have ended, I find myself approaching turbaned strangers in public and wishing them healing and hope. It is a sister- and brotherhood, wearing your cancer publicly. Suddenly you find yourself in an almost secret society, all of whom are passing for "OK" in the larger world.

At the same time that I felt this heartfelt connection to total strangers, I heard from many friends battling cancer that they suddenly felt distanced from family and friends. This is a phenomenon I've heard over the years. In some instances, friends and family don't know what to do when they hear your diagnosis, and so they turn their faces toward something else, something less terrifying. "Next year, when you're well, we'll do this or that." "Do you think you'll be up to getting together in six months?" My friend Margaret found during her cancer that once some people heard her diagnosis, they treated her as if she were "pre-dead." There are people who get so freaked out by your diagnosis, they back away, murmuring bland or superstitious incantations. "I'm sure this will be fine," "God never gives us more than we can handle," "Call me when you're feeling up to it. . ." And then, they run.

I believe in the power of Love. Throughout my priesthood, I've collected articles and research findings about health and healing, and the power of relationships. I believe in every cell of my body that our friendships and relationships are holy, and that the practice of sharing our hearts with one another is the sacred work we are called to do in this life. The fact that healing—mental, spiritual, and physical healing—happens as well because of these connections is no surprise to me. We are all connected.

This belief made my diagnosis especially ill-timed. That first week of June, I looked around at my life in Burlington, at the local friendships and connections I had forged in a year, and came up fairly empty handed. My classmates in the M.S. program in communication science and disorders at the University of Vermont had all, just the week before, scattered to various summer programs around the country, doing our required internship in swallowing disorders at hospitals and care centers. (The fact that I, too, had been hired to take an internship position that had suddenly fallen through and left me open for the summer. . . well, let's just say the time and space to do my treatment without working at the same time was a huge gift.)

My other group of friends was the choir at the Episcopal cathedral where I sang, but that week had been our final Sunday, and now the choir was off until the fall. My family was in Baltimore and Virginia. My husband lived in New Hampshire. I wanted to do my treatment in Burlington, but I knew that having nobody there to lean on was not good. The hospital offered social workers, and thank God for my therapist whose work with me was going to help me walk through my cancer treatment in hopeful, open, curious directions. . . but as for friends, I was down to a very few, and I was loathe to over-burden them.

So I hatched what now sounds like a crazy plan. First, let me explain something about myself. I am someone who absolutely loves eating out alone. Crazy ethnic places, comforting diners, French bistros—I thrive on the ambiance and chattering, as I sit in a corner savoring my food, reading a book, and just soaking in the sound and sensations. Even though I am generally an enthusiastic and talkative person, my inner introvert loves sitting alone in public places. And, if that public place happens to have strong coffee, an eclectic draft beer selection, or a fine red wine, well, who am I to say no?

Where could I go, I wondered to myself, at almost any hour of any day, if I'm feeling ratty or discouraged? Whom could I rely on to be there for me instantly, when I needed someone nonjudgmental and encouraging?

Of course. Out of the blue it came to me: the waitresses at the Athens Diner. Yes, I know it sounds crazy, but alone in my apartment the week after I was diagnosed with cancer, I chose the waitstaff at my favorite diner to become my family during my cancer journey. The only thing remaining was for me to tell them.

I was a familiar face at the Athens Diner, though a fairly new one. Nevertheless, in that magical fashion of the best diners, I had felt at home from my first visit. Sitting alone in my booth, I had loved the gals joking with other diners from behind the counter, or hollering orders through the tiny window into the kitchen, or calling to a server in the back room, "Yeah—we're out of the pecan pie, Lois, but the maple walnut looks better anyway—" In a former life, I'd waited tables myself, and had learned a lot about my own shortcomings that way. I had been a cheerful but absentminded waitress. It is a true gift to serve tables, and not a gift I possess, and so my affection for these ladies was met by my deep respect for their effortless ballet of service.

They must have been psychic as well as competent. In one of those beautiful "life imitating art" ways, they could tell you what you needed or wanted, and were not shy about it. I might think I was going to have the spanakopita, but Ruth would look searchingly into my face and say, "You know, I think you should have the Reuben instead—OK?" She was always exactly right.

On this June morning, I went to the diner to tell them. They were, after my real family, the first people I told I had cancer. I timed my trip for just after the breakfast rush, when I knew Ruth and Esther and Megan and Abby and Ashley would get a little time to snag their own breakfasts, and would have more time to really talk.

Sitting sideways in my booth, with my feet on the banquette and my back against the wall so I could face the counter, I ordered the vegetarian skillet breakfast and waited. When the few other straggling diners had left, except for one old fellow at the counter reading the paper and drinking coffee, I called the gals over.

"Hey—I just got some bad news, and I need to tell you—" Immediately, they leaned in, two plopping down in the booth with me, and the others gathering around. "Cricket, what? Are you OK, honey?"

"No, I'm not. I just found out I have cancer."

The eruption was enormous. This was the first time I'd told anyone in person. Tears welled in their eyes, and Ashley shoved my feet off the seat so she could scoot next to me, and put her arm around me. Questions exploded out of them: What kind? Is it breast? What stage? How do you feel? What can we do? What can we do? *What can we do*?

And, for the first time since the diagnosis, I burst into tears and was able to bury my face in the shoulder of a friend. The tears felt good, but as the first flow of sadness drained from me, I found myself edging closer to the fear.

Fighting my own fear was like riding waves of the ocean. Ups and downs, gentle rolling motions and then dramatic crashes. My biggest crash was the day of the bone marrow extraction. I must have seen something on TV when I was young about the procedure, and was terrified of it happening to me. When I asked Gianni if I would be knocked out during that, he said, "Oh no, it's done with just a local anesthesia. It doesn't take much time at all."

I wasn't worried about the time, however. I was worried about the pain. I asked him if I might get some sort of anxiety-relief medication before and during the procedure, and he smiled kindly. "Absolutely. You can have whatever you need to make this easy on you."

The morning of the extraction, I was trying my best to keep focused on my breathing, to calm myself down. Trying to stay "in the moment," however, wasn't helping, since I found myself in a moment I did not want to be in. When my nurse came to give me a quick hug and wish me well, I asked her if she would go find the prescription meds for me. "Oh, I can't. You aren't allowed anything until after you've signed all the consent forms." Fair enough; they wouldn't want me all relaxed and happy when I was signing off on the list of possible side effects or unforeseen issues that might go awry. I breathed more deeply, and waited some more.

The next woman into the room had to start a deep IV in my arm. Would she run out and get me the drugs, please? No, she was from phlebotomy, not pharmacy. Then came the official forms to sign, giving them permission to drill into the back of my hip, insert a syringe, and extract marrow. Whew. The papers were signed, and I was ready for LaLaLand. Except when they came in to prep me, I asked once more for the drugs, and they tried to talk me out of them. "Yes," said one nurse, "I see the scrip here, but you don't want that stuff. You won't be able to drive home for hours if you have it." Driving home was honestly not on my list of worries. I'd gladly snooze in the waiting room for the rest of the day, if I could only have my anxiety dialed down a bit. The next staff person had barely gotten through the door into the room before I unhinged and launched myself at her. Begging, starting to cry, I asked again for the Valium or whatever they'd ordered for me, so I wouldn't have to feel my rising terror of the procedure. This woman started to cry, too, at my distress, and hugged me tightly to her chest, while she whispered in my ear, "Honey, I'm just here to empty the trash cans. But I'll go find someone to help you." Two minutes later, a nurse came in with a handful of vials and gave me the meds. As for the extraction itself? It didn't hurt a bit. Yes, it was odd and frightening, but staying in the moment worked. Other than many, many shots of Lidocaine to numb the small of my back, where the harvesting took place, and the feeling of pressure as they drilled a hole through the back of my hip bone, the procedure was not painful. Only the waiting hurt.

When you work to let go of the fear, the journey offers up countless moments of surprise, or peace, or joy, or total hilarity. For example, there was the surprise ultrasound. My starting date for chemo got bumped a few days, when Gianni ordered more tests.[6] After having been through the PET scans and the CT scans, and survived the infamous bone marrow extraction, I was sent early the next Monday morning to the basement of the hospital for what is called a transvaginal ultrasound. A handy brochure from the waiting room described this procedure:

> A specially designed ultrasound probe is used for this procedure. It will be covered with a protective sheath and lubricating gel, then gently inserted into your vagina. The ultrasound probe will need to be moved in different positions in order to visualize the uterus and ovaries clearly.

Well, there you have it. What could be simpler?

I showed up at 8 am, resigned to another weirdly invasive procedure. Trying to be curious. *Let's not label this.* The tech who was going to be scanning me was very young, and over-the-top bubbly and cheerful. She peppered me with questions while setting up her instrumentation. Did I need the bathroom? Was the room warm enough? And the inevitable Vermont small-talk question, was I putting in a garden that summer? I wondered if the chatter was her way of coping with the intrusiveness of the situation, or perhaps she felt a close bond to all women, since she spent all day, every day, wandering around inside their bodies?

In any event, I was quickly half naked and "assumed the position" on the scanning table, as for a pelvic exam. She had discreetly left me alone to get settled and to pull a sheet over my knees. The table was padded and comfy, and I was telling myself that there was nothing to

---

6. Specifically, he was checking to be certain that the cancer was contained in one half of my body, as defined by my diaphragm. Cancer that appears and stays in one half is a stage 1 or 2, but a cancer that has traveled across this boundary is a stage 3 or 4.

fear, that this was simply another exam not unlike others I'd had. "Be curious" was becoming my mantra, even if I couldn't actually achieve that curiosity. At least I knew what I was working toward.

The tech returned and talked me through the basic procedure. When she was finished, she asked whether I'd prefer inserting the scanning device myself, or have her do it. For the first time, I looked over to the examining table and saw The Device.

Holy Mother of God—the thing looked like a fallen oak tree. I'm not kidding. Maybe looked like a giant redwood. Not comfortingly, it had a large handle on its far end.

Her question hung in the air between us. What was preferable, trying to find room for this monstrous thing inside my body by myself, or allowing a trained professional to do this? Is there another choice?

"Be curious. . . be curious." I was trying desperately to remind myself. My curiosity was fast failing me.

Flash forward past the most awkward moment of my life, and now the Redwood was in place, with the tech grabbing the handle. Honestly, watching her maneuver it was like watching an Indy 500 driver shifting quickly through the gears. First, second, third—hold. . . then she would press inwards or press up or down, as if shifting into reverse or overdrive, as she clicked away with her free hand on her ultrasound monitor, catching whatever objects of interest she seemed to be locating. I felt a fresh kinship with the interior of my car, and vowed only to shift ever so gently for the rest of my life.

It was at this point that she chirped brightly, "So, have you read *50 Shades of Grey*?"

This, my friends, was an excruciatingly funny moment. I mean, really. If I could have burst out laughing while the Giant Redwood felt like it was bumping into my tonsils, I sure would have.

This was the summer of that book, and it was a common enough question among pals over drinks at the pub, but here? I looked over, to see if she were indeed making a joke, realizing the utter incongruity of chatting about this soft-porn novel while exploring my interior parts with an enormous probe. She seemed totally oblivious.

Meanwhile, since I hadn't read the book, she felt compelled to describe it to me, all the time innocently shifting from reverse to fifth gear over and over. I stared at the ceiling and chuckled.

You really can't miss if you just show up in your own life and stay curious.

CHEMO ROUND ONE

I was so glad that Tom and my sister Cathy had come to Vermont to be with me for my first round of chemo. The day before it began, I was summoned to the hospital for "chemo class," an introduction to the treatment. My nurse, Kristen, had a trainee with her, a nurse who would be learning the ropes for teaching the Introduction to Chemotherapy class in the future. Since my sister had gotten to town a few days earlier, I dragged her with me.

Sitting in one of those faux-cheery consulting rooms, Kristen started to explain the technical aspects of the chemo. She described the precise drugs that I would be receiving: Rituximab, Doxorubicin, Vincristine and Cyclophosphamide, Prednisone, on and on the list went, until she mentioned an anti-emetic called Ondansetron.

As Coopers, my sister and I have both been well-trained to find something funny in almost every life situation. Sometimes it's a shield, and sometimes it's simply for our own amusement. So when we heard the word "Ondansetron," Cathy and I, in the same breath, got the giggles. It reminded me of the Christmas poem, and I turned to her and whispered, "On Dancetron! On Dashetron! On Donner and Blitzatron!" She, meanwhile, thought "Danc-e-tron" sounded like a dance move, and started humming something back to me that sounded alarmingly like the BeeGees from *Saturday Night Fever.*

Kristen finally had to stop talking, because Cathy and I were gasping for breath, tears flowing down our faces, our giggles having turned to full-body gales of laughter. The trainee nurse watched, worriedly, as Kristen whispered to her, "This is. . . um. . . pretty unusual. As a rule, they just sit there quietly. . ." It looked like the trainee wanted to call for a psych consult. Cathy and I, however, were snorting and trying to pull ourselves together. "Sorry, sorry," I gasped, "Go on. That just struck me as funny. . ." I babbled lamely.

The chemo class was just a warm-up for the "cancer sex" class. The river of chemicals racing through my body would create all sorts of changes, many of which would not be predictable. In particular, mucus membranes can become decidedly affected, whether they are in your mouth, your alimentary canal, your excretory system, or, well, other places.

The chemo-sex coach came in after Kristen and her stunned trainee left. She was elderly and sweet, and very compassionate, but honestly that day—the day before I started chemo—my sex life was not on my top ten list of concerns. Still, I took notes and tried to be a good student, if only to honor her sincerity and dedication.

When I recounted this educational offering to my Mindfulness in Health Care class several months later, we joked about inventing a chemo version of Match.com. "Welcome to Chemo Hookups. Temporary matches for your treatment months." "Upload your photo today: We're all bald!" Although we doubled over with laughter, something about the idea remains deeply touching to me. So many folks are single or have partners who can't cope with the cancer. How wonderful to have someone *simpatico* at the end of the day to share treatment stories and then even dinner and bedtime? I think the mental health part of our insurance really ought to cover this.

One of the ways that I prepared myself for the first round of chemo was to pack kind of a day bag like you would for a trip to the beach, only without the beer.

I had had a quick tour of the chemo suite and was terrified. I couldn't have known that it was an unusual day, but most of the folks there who being infused were very ill. My heart broke open time and time again, as each four-patient pod of the suite offered up patient after patient, curled into him- or herself under layers of blankets. This is you in a few months, my mind kept thinking. This is your future. No—stop. Stay in *this* moment.

I decided to prepare by packing. They told me that the liquids used in the infusions would be either at room temperature or a tad cooler, and they can make you feel downright chilly as your body absorbs them, so I packed a comfy blanket and a travel pillow, as if I were off on an overnight flight to Europe.

Of course, the terror is that the chemo will produce uncontrollable vomiting. That was the image I had, anyway, from the past few decades of hearing about the process. (I won't leave you worrying here: mine is a completely vomit-free story.) Still, the idea of food was a scary one—what will feel OK in my tummy? What will stay down, and what will not? My mom had sent me a care package containing an assortment of ginger items, as ginger naturally soothes an upset stomach, so I had my ginger gum and ginger hard candies tucked into my bag. I had been warned that a chemo day was long (the first one was about ten hours). I would need to eat something, sooner or later.

Tom and Cathy would be spending the day with me, so I didn't expect to be bored, but I tucked a few books into my pack, especially Pema Chödrön's *The Places That Scare You: A Guide to Fearlessness in Difficult Times*. Also my knitting, and an iPod and earbuds.

I had put together a playlist on my iPod to listen to during chemo. I compiled hours of unrelated music, from the Beatles' cheerful "Here Comes the Sun" and sweet "Today" by John Denver, to the funny Weird Al's "Amish Paradise" and the groovy "Element Chant" by Spiral Rhythm. After some thought, I titled the playlist: Chemical Warfare. OK, I was ready. Bring it on.

Arriving for chemo day one was disconcerting. I felt great, physically, so it was counterintuitive knowing the drugs themselves would make me feel sick. After three weeks of scans and meetings and invasive procedures, looking at my x-rays, PET scans, CT scans, still it was hard for me truly to believe that there was a fist-sized mass growing between my heart and right lung, just hovering in there. Walking into the chemo suite seemed wrong, somehow.

My new port was ready in my chest, surgically tucked under the top layer of skin, but the glued-shut incision was still fresh and sore. Kristen explained to me that the chemicals are so caustic, a course of chemo would cause severe damage to the veins during an infusion. This new system, with the bottle-cap-sized port in the chest, from which a tiny IV tube was snaked under my skin, up to my throat, slid into my jugular, and then snaked through the jugular down into the superior vena cava vein, which pumps blood directly into the right atrium of the heart, was intended to avoid that particular damage.

While she was calmly explaining all of this to me, I was mentally hitting the brakes. "Hey, wait a minute here. The drugs are so nasty they'll destroy my veins, so the 'better' option is to stick them straight into my heart? My *heart*, for crying out loud? Hello? Anyone else think this is freaking nuts?"

Kristen watched me flip out with her usual patience. She acted as if I were the only patient she'd ever had, and that she had never explained a treatment before—everything was gently tailored to my personal experience. "Yes," she said, "yes, it does sound stupid, doesn't it? But here is why it's also genius."

This upper right chamber of the heart is like a tropical getaway. Imagine a secret hot tub with a gorgeous cascading waterfall splashing down from above. Mmmmm, this chamber of the heart is like a tiny spa vacation in your chest. This is where there is the largest concentration of blood all in one spot, so that the drugs are immediately diluted as much as possible. "OK," my brain conceded, "that sounds good." It is also a fast-moving area, because that chamber is pumping blood out just as quickly as it is filling up, so if you drip the chemo drugs into the waterfall, and they splash down into the hot tub, they are also quickly mixed with the blood and pumped out into the rest of the body. No waiting around for a long trip through the veins, burning everything along the way. The caustic drugs get mixed with lots of blood fast, and are on their way quickly to find those cancer cells and kill them off. By the end of her explanation, I was convinced. "Let's do this," I said.

The suite I was in was well designed. It was broken up into groups of four infusion stations, and each pod was your little chemo universe. There was a recliner chair for the patient, a chair or two for visitors, all the necessary medical apparatus, a table, a mini-TV, and a curtain for privacy. Once hooked up to the IV, I also had the option of grabbing my IV pole and wandering a little bit around the larger area, using the bathroom, checking out the snacks in the two small kitchens, visiting with others, looking out the windows, and so forth. We were allowed to roll ourselves to the end of the linoleum, but where the carpet started we had to stop. It felt a little bit like electric fencing for dogs.

My nurse was seasoned and no-nonsense, but she was also intensely committed to making sure my first day went well. I felt deeply cared for, as she took all the time I needed to talk and answer questions throughout the day. Also, being a first-timer meant I got the chair by the window, which afforded a little extra privacy as well as a stunning view of the gardens outside, designed for the very purpose of delighting people in the chemo suite, whether you were inside getting infused or able to step outside. Little touches like this garden helped in ways that are hard to articulate; it was a reminder of beauty, and the knowledge that strangers cared enough to design, build, and maintain a garden to delight patients. It was another reminder that a chemo journey is supported by innumerable hands, that each of us had a community around us, visible and invisible.

Propped in my chair, playlist booted up and ready, Tom and Cathy beside me, nervously waiting, I sat as the nurse started to hook up a fat IV bag of bright red liquid. She explained to us that the Rituxan often caused an allergic reaction, and so I should pay attention to how I was feeling, and signal to her if I felt anything out of the ordinary. The drip was set at a glacial pace, and I watched it head down the tubing toward my heart.

Every now and then, as I continued to tolerate the infusion, my nurse would check my vital signs and then let me know she was turning up the speed of the drip. After about the fourth time, she said, "Okay, we are now in the region when most people will experience side effects, so I'll be close by. Remember to grab me if anything at all seems to change in your body." She was hooking up an IV on a fellow across from me, so even though I didn't think I'd need her, she was reassuringly close.

Then everything happened so fast, it was hard to separate the different actions. Tom and Cathy and I were chatting away when suddenly I felt an intense itching on my uvula. I mused that I'd never felt that before, and then it hit me, *allergic reaction*. In the half second it took me to think that thought, I could feel my soft palate begin to swell and fall downward into the back of my throat. My nurse flew to my side, stopping the IV and immediately pushing Benadryl into my line. She also must have sent out some kind of alarm, because the next thing I knew, my chair had been tipped way back and I was surrounded by clinicians, nurses, and doctors. Through a bit of a fog, I could see Tom and Cathy, now pushed against the far wall, anxiously watching the buzz of medical activity.

The curtains had been drawn around me, but they fluttered as different people seemed to be peeking in. I could hear voices asking, "Who was it? Oh. That one in the chair? She looks OK." Then Gianni was pulling up a chair beside me, smiling. "How are you feeling?" he murmured. I wanted to tell him that if this was how day one was going to go down, I was suddenly taking this chemo much more seriously. That's not what came out, though, because my face didn't really seem to be attached to anything I could manipulate with my brain. I had been given such a wallop of Benadryl, I think I kept falling asleep during the questioning.

Eventually, with me still breathing and everything else having calmed down, the nurse explained that she could now turn the IV up full speed, since the reaction I had had would now prevent another reaction from occurring. Through my earbuds, Carole King was singing something about being far away; I agreed with her and fell back into a groggy sleep.

The rest of the drugs dripped without drama, taking so long that my nurse's shift ended and the only employees left in the chemo suite were a night-shift nurse and the folks mopping the floors. Finally I was unhooked and given sheets of directives for being in touch over the next few days. I'd already filled my prescriptions for the many drugs I needed at home, and Cathy, Tom, and I wearily wandered out of the hospital, leaving behind the sound of industrial vacuum cleaners.

Out on the sidewalk, we agreed we were ravenous. I was worried about eating, but we hadn't really had a decent meal all day. Nearby was a good Italian restaurant; we got a table there and ordered up plates piled high with food, talking perhaps a little too loudly in order to shake off the worry of the day. I wondered if I looked different on the outside. I couldn't believe that I could be pumped full of so much poison and still look exactly the same.

We headed back to my apartment. My tiny bedroom had an attached bathroom, but my information sheets said that for the next eighteen weeks, I should not share a bathroom with anyone if at all possible, because my bodily fluids could be classified as hazardous materials. Talk about feeling a little creepy being inside your own body. Tom and Cathy made up beds on the couches in the living room, and went to brush their teeth in the bathrooms in the hallway outside.

Fully exhausted, I dropped into bed and soon fell asleep. In the middle of the night, I woke up, wondering what it was that had roused me. Oh. *Oh.* I realized that my large dinner actually was not settling very well, and I was starting to feel queasy. Growing waves of nausea seemed to be ebbing and flowing inside of me. I swallowed hard, and reached for the information sheets on the bedside table to go through my checklists; I realized that I'd forgotten to take one of the Ondancetron tablets before bed. Whoops. I went to the bathroom, chose the right bottle from my array, and swallowed down the tiny pill. That done, I went back to bed, marveling that before I was fully horizontal, the nausea had completely vanished. I was asleep again in moments.

The next day dawned, uncharacteristically hot and humid. Cathy, Tom, and I mostly napped in front of the fan throughout the day. Was everything really OK, or would I at any moment become ragingly ill? Kristen called midmorning to check on me, and I told her that the only thing I felt was hot and sticky from the weather.

My mom called, expecting to hear a worried report about how sick I felt, and was not quite certain we were being honest as each one of us told her I was feeling fine. My sister finally had to step into the hallway out of earshot of me to prove that she was indeed telling the truth. The next day was the same, and the next. I took my pills, I waited and watched, but each day I felt unpredictably OK.

I bumped into Gianni in the hospital hallway one afternoon about a week after the chemo day. He scanned my face, and said he thought I looked surprisingly well. I told him I'd been wondering if my having been a theatre person and (dare I say it) drinking alcohol in no small quantities throughout my teen and early college years had perhaps, in some way, conditioned my body to being cyclically poisoned and bouncing back? He tipped his head back and laughed out loud. "You know," he said, "it's a theory. The folks who seem to have the worst time of it are the ones who have never had any alcohol, never had any strong drugs before. They tend to get very sick. I don't know how you might continue to test this theory, but who knows? You might be on to something." Chuckling to himself, he squeezed my arm and then strode off to his next consultation.

It was also in these first weeks that my friend Joan, of the Cellmates, started to send me quick photos every day of something beautiful. Often, it was a flower. Occasionally, it might be a vista, or something in her yard. Not a big deal, not any huge message, just the photo. But they started coming every day. It was genius. When I least expected it, there would come some tiny reminder that a friend far away was thinking of me, was sending me a little cheer so that I wouldn't feel alone. My heart swelled each time. Meanwhile, other gifts and delights came my way. I can't recall who sent me the small pig that shot Nerf balls out of its nose, but it was a huge favorite in the chemo suite. The smallest things could light up my day, giving me pleasure for hours or days.

As I continued to meditate and read more books about how to unhook from unsatisfying patterns of living, I found my spirit growing lighter, and my heart for all people growing larger. Looking at anyone while out in public—man, woman, or child—could reduce me to tears. A curl of hair at the nape of a neck, a dirty Band-Aid on a chubby finger, a quick look exchanged between friends—all these things were noticed, and cherished, as I found myself freshly alive in the family of humans.

I found that I could greet each day with unconditional gratitude. Since I didn't know how long my good luck was going to last, I tried to get outside and enjoy the sunshine, and imagined that the sun was also working its healing on me from the outside in. I had been warned not to stay out in the sun too long, as the drugs would make me hypersensitive to sunlight, but it felt so good that it was hard to monitor myself.

I also bought myself a treat, a Toronto Maple Leafs jersey. That very first day, when the doctor at Student Health was explaining what non-Hodgkin's lymphoma was, he kept saying "NHL" over and over. I admit to having been in a total fog of denial at the time, but I truly wondered why he kept mentioning the National Hockey League.

Weston Priory

My first true pilgrimage had taken place forty-two years earlier, on April 22, 1970, the first Earth Day. I don't know how it had been publicized so that even I, a second grader, caught onto the idea. Somehow, I got it into my head that I had to walk to school that morning. My mother, permissive with my flights of fancy (though I would like to imagine she had been swayed by an eight-year-old's passion for saving the earth), allowed me to get up well before dawn that day and take to the streets—alone—for a three-mile journey I had never walked before. We hadn't clocked it out, though I had drawn a crude map of where to turn and on which streets, and I remember stepping out into the dark morning, tingling with nervous excitement (and with the chilly air), and setting my sights toward school, as awe inspiring as the Matterhorn to a second grader.

It wasn't at all clear to me, when I arrived, why the doors were all locked. Had school begun without me? Just how long had the walk taken? I was disoriented, cold, and needed to use the bathroom. The fact that my school was *ever* locked was astonishing to me as I waited for someone to arrive and open the front doors.

As far as pilgrimages go, it might not have been very exciting, but I'll never forget the stages of it, the determined inevitability beforehand of knowing that I *had* to make the journey. The planning (picture a map in crayon on a dinner-sized paper napkin.) The choices and surprises along the way. The sense of triumph when I arrived, immediately followed by intense questioning: "What was that about? Why did I do it? What did it mean?"

Deep within each one of us, there is a secret longing. Some people long for the open sea. Some people long for the tops of mountains. Some people long for the jostle and clamor of Times Square. The point isn't that we long for different things, but rather that we all share this experience of longing.

These deep longings aren't explicable. We may or may not be able to trace the roots of them. They are woven through our dreams and the very fabric of our hearts. Can you remember sitting by the window on a perfect spring day in high school or college, the fresh, fragrant breeze from outside drawing your imagination out and beyond, the singing in your soul calling, "Away, away"?

I'm the one who couldn't ignore the call. I'm the one who jumped from the window (more than once) when the teacher's back was turned, leaving my open books on the desk. I'm the one who once crawled with Christa, a college friend and co-conspirator, around a table and out of a class discussion of *Don Quixote* because, well, why talk about a quest when you could leave on one?

I don't know why I have always longed to be on pilgrimage; I just know that this is so. And the funny thing is, I don't much like going for a walk. What I long for are journeys, challenges, a little mix of fear and surprise, the opportunity to rely on myself and my wits alone. No, I am not a thrill seeker. I do not long for danger, for severe physical discomfort, for jumping out of planes, wrestling wild animals, battling Mother Nature, or engaging in extreme sports. I eschew rollercoasters, scary movies, heights (if I can help it), and physical risks. I do not like to be terrified.

But a spiritual journey? Especially one that has history or challenge, involves some sacrifice, and that may have the potential to draw me closer to the great mysteries? Count me in. My bag is always packed.

In those limbo weeks between the diagnosis and the start of chemo, I may have thrown myself into the pilgrimage planning as a way to place touchstones in the future. I can't be dead in August, right? I have these reservations at a monastery, after all.

I also knew that I would need to be repeatedly drawn out of my naturally hermetic inclinations. It is a familiar struggle in my life to stay connected to people. I need to be pulled into relationships, into community, or I fear that left to my own devices I would end up in some cabin in the woods, living in my thoughts for the rest of my life. This was just one reason to find community during the chemo months—precisely because I knew my own inclination would be to hole up like a squirrel and never see anyone.

Perhaps this is a hint of my call to the priesthood. I have somehow always known that I had to hitch myself, vocationally, to the world. Maybe God could see my solitary nature and knew I would need to be connected, for life, to the people around me. Good call, God.

In any event, I wanted to go on pilgrimage to holy sites or monasteries of different faith traditions to search for healing, to surround myself with people of prayer, to experience and learn for myself new ways to lift up my heart in different traditions, and to have regularly scheduled opportunities to get the heck out of town. However, having not started chemo yet, I didn't have any idea how I would feel or what sorts of side effects I might experience. So I decided to draw a five-hour driving radius around Burlington on a map and travel to places within that circle. There was no magic to that number. I love to drive, so a three-hour trip feels like a warm-up to me. Five hours felt like a real distance, but also seemed close enough to make it back to the hospital if I needed help fast.

I had to refine the circle a bit. From northern Vermont, the circle was almost half filled by Canada. I dearly love nosing through the shops in Montreal or examining ice sculptures in Quebec City.

Nevertheless, though I explored some options north of the border, I was nervous about being in another country with an unpredictable medical condition. If my health went south fast, did I really want to risk having to be admitted to a hospital in another country? Then there would be the awkwardness of crossing the border with a back-pack full of powerful prescription drugs. Tempted as I was to keep Canadian options open, I realized I wasn't going to be comfortable pushing the envelope quite that far. This decision made, I turned my gaze to what was left. The circle encompassed all of Vermont, New Hampshire and Connecticut, a good chunk of Maine, all but a shred of Rhode Island, most of Massachusetts, and upstate New York almost to Rochester in the west and not quite all the way to New York City heading south.

From here, I just started googling. "Retreat Center," "Monastery," "Buddhist," "Zen," "Orthodox," "Sacred." As website after website loaded, I could see a different journey unfolding—not the chemo journey I so feared, but instead a summer filled with the peace prom-ised by the websites of countless holy places. Wide expanses of lawn, mountaintop vistas, the shining floors of meditation halls, tiny ascetic sleeping rooms. . . it was all perfect. They were all perfect.

Quite often, places like this are very welcoming to the visitor, the seeker, and the pilgrim. Some of them have regularly scheduled retreats; others are monastic houses where individuals are invited to come for peace and prayer on their own. Most of them specify that they do not expect guests to share their tradition, but that all are welcome to join them whatever their spiritual inclinations—or lack thereof—might be. And almost all of them are easily affordable, even for an unemployed graduate student like me.

My plan was to set up pilgrimages in the third week of each three-week chemo cycle. That would give me two weeks to clear the chemi-cals out of my body, and hopefully to bounce back from the treatment enough to enjoy the drives and the experiences. The internet (which of course I was *not* consulting about my cancer) seemed to indicate that a person should feel better by the end of the cycle, and thus able to go into the next chemo treatment ready for another dose.

All that was left was to make a list of the most enticing options, and check their calendars to see if the weeks I was looking for retreat time matched openings they had. Quickly, I had many more than I needed for my six rounds.

Next was to choose a spectrum of differing traditions, to have the pilgrimages span a breadth of religious and spiritual expression. I wanted to be pulled and stretched, I wanted to go to some familiar places, and some that would be challenging. Quickly I created a list and began contacting the people on the other side of the websites. The dates and availability and cost all fell into place.

Now that I had my chemo schedule and my pilgrimage schedule, I felt ready for whatever lay ahead.

> *Spirit of New Life, Spirit of our God,*
> *Come and breathe within us,*
> *Come and be our song, Alleluia!*
>
> —the monks of Weston Priory

I chose Weston Priory to be my first pilgrimage because I had been there before, almost thirty years earlier. I moved to Vermont right out of college, looking for ways to connect to the land, to myself, and to God. At the time, the monks of Weston Priory were known both for their music and for their political activism.

The early 1980s were the beginnings of the Sanctuary Movement. Central Americans, fleeing civil wars in El Salvador and Guatemala or the results of revolution in Nicaragua, headed north over the Mexican border for safety. However, immigration laws at the time were not hospitable to them. Quietly, a network of religious communities throughout the United States and Canada offered themselves as "sanctuaries," safe places where refugees could find shelter, work, legal aid, and eventually a new home.

The brothers of Weston Priory, a Roman Catholic monastic community in the hills of Vermont, had adopted one of the refugee families in defiance of federal law. I was first drawn to the community because I loved their music, joyful and hope-filled, with simple, spare guitar accompaniment. However, as I learned more about the community, I realized that it was the first time I'd thought of monks as political activists. I was stunned by their courage, taking the teachings of the gospel so seriously that they actually patterned their lives by them. I had been a churchgoer my entire life, and Roman Catholic for the first sixteen years, but it had not yet occurred to me that taking one's faith seriously meant actually ordering one's life in risky, countercultural ways. I was smitten by the monks' passion, and drawn to them with a deep longing. Fresh out of college, I visited Weston Priory and it became a retreat home for me, as I better articulated my own call to the Episcopal priesthood.

In August 1985, a year before I left Vermont to go to seminary, the monks sponsored a 93-mile "Walk for Peace and Justice," highlighting Vermont's two Central American sanctuaries, a walk that followed the old Underground Railroad route. The walk began at Weston Priory and ended, days later, at Christ Church Presbyterian parish in Burlington, a community that had also adopted a family from Central America. Inspired by the monks' witness, I signed up to walk the whole distance, stopping for rallies and concerts and sleeping in barns and gyms along the way. In the early 1980s, I had felt deeply rooted in the love and hope of these monks and so, following my diagnosis, I knew that this time of crisis and healing was a perfect time to return to them.

The Benedictine community's largest public festival of the year is their annual worship and picnic in honor of St. Benedict. Hundreds of people of every faith, and of no faith, flock to the priory on that summer Saturday, to honor a saint remembered for his generous understanding of hospitality. I had attended this celebration in my early twenties, and delighted especially in the outdoor folk dancing.

As a visitor, the vision of these joyful men in their monastic robes cavorting around a field, hand in hand with their guests, is not easily forgotten.

Was it coincidence, or a deep, universal *welcome home*, that aligned my first pilgrimage dates with this annual festival for St. Benedict? Guest rooms for the event were generally spoken for long in advance, but when I called in June to set up my visit a few weeks later, one room had just opened up. I would be there for St. Benedict's Day.

Two days before I left on this first pilgrimage, I woke up and sat on the edge of my bed, taking my temperature. This daily ritual was to track any sign of a fever, since lymphoma is a cancer of the white blood cells, a cancer living in your immune system. Since the chemo was killing off these cells, a patient had to be extra vigilant about ordinary colds or germs because the immune system was compromised during treatment, making it difficult to fight off even a run-of-the-mill sniffle.

While I waited for the thermometer to beep, I glanced down at the unmade bed, and noticed a dark stain on my pillowcase. My glasses were still on the bedside table, so I reached for them and looked back down. Huh. I reached over, and picked up the pillow, and the "stain" fell off onto the sheets. It wasn't a stain at all. It was a pile of my hair.

Even when you are expecting this to happen, it's a shock. I reached down and picked up the scattered strands, feeling their weight and number. Nervously, I raised one hand to the back of my head to feel for a bald patch, but so far, there seemed to be at least a covering of hair across my whole head. Curiously, I found myself pinching a few strands of hair on my head between my fingers and giving a little tug. No resistance at all, and they were in my hand as well.

Immediately after I was diagnosed, my nurse had handed me a prescription for a wig. Many types of insurance will cover some, if not all, of the cost of a wig. Curiously, the coverage is found under mental health needs and the wig is justified just as though it were a prosthetic arm or leg. A wig is referred to as a "cranial prosthesis," replacing your hair like a missing limb, and prescribed in order to ease the grief and anguish of the loss of this body part.

I found this fascinating. I wasn't entirely horrified at the thought of losing my hair since the trade-off, hopefully, was not dying. Kristen had urged me to "run, not walk" to the local wig maker, before I even started chemo, so she could match color and style and have it ready when my hair began to fall out. I had gone immediately to the local stylist, who made a full-time job out of creating wigs, and had found talking with her to be one of the most surprising visits in those early weeks.

Diane, who owned and ran her own shop, enfolded me like a sister. Her samples of hair literally covered every inch of all four walls of an entire room. It was a slightly itchy feeling, being in a room that was wallpapered from ceiling to floor in hanks of hair, something like a cross between a padded cell and the lair of some serial killer. Of course, Diane couldn't have been kinder, but I had to swallow an urge to take a hairbrush and brush one of her walls.

Sitting me in her stylist chair, she asked me every question under the sun about my hair. How did I wear it (shoved impatiently behind my ears), how much time did I like to devote to styling it (thirty seconds), and was I interested in something new and different during these months or would I like her to create something that matched my current hairstyle and color (match). I didn't have any frame of reference for wigs, other than the kind elderly relatives had in the 1960s, which were basically thick rubber swim caps with hair sewn or glued to them. They had been heavy, smelly, sweaty—I wasn't really convinced that I would end up wearing a wig, but I had committed to staying open to everything that was offered.

What Diane showed me, however, was unrelated in almost every way from those old models. These were all custom-made on lightweight, airy caps of a gauze-like material that was thin and breathable. Diane showed me how she used something very like a crochet hook to attach just a few strands at a time to the base, creating hair that would fall precisely the way I liked it to. The base layer is so thin that when you part your new hair, the skin you see is your actual scalp showing through. It was miraculous, and I got a boost just hearing her enthusiasm and watching what she was going to create for me. The creating of it would take several weeks, so after much measuring and matching of swatches to my natural hair color, she sent me off with a hug to await its completion.

That morning, sitting on the edge of my bed, I still had a little over a week to wait for the wig. I had bought a few of those "chemo kerchief" scarves online, and so I dug through my box of chemo supplies, found the fabric triangles, and tied one on. Going into the bathroom, I checked myself in the mirror. Not too bad—I looked like someone getting ready for a day of cleaning house. The back of it flapped down enough to cover what I was certain would be a large bald patch by that very night.

The chemo made my scalp feel as though I had a bad sunburn. It had started about a week after the infusion, and now at the two-week point, my head was prickly and sore all the time, with hair that suddenly felt so fragile I was afraid to brush it that morning, for fear that the hairbrush would pull it all out. Looking into the mirror again, I admitted to myself that my first real emotion after the shock of seeing the hair on my pillow was a deep sense of relief. Because I had not felt seriously ill after the chemo dose, there was some tiny piece of my brain that worried that perhaps they'd somehow mixed up my meds and I'd only gotten an infusion of saline or something that wasn't going to work. Feeling oddly healthy even following the first round of chemo was, for me, a tad worrying.

But now, here was proof. If my hair was falling out, then, yes, I *had* had chemo! It was odd to feel relieved, but it was affirmation that we were fighting this cancer, and I felt strangely better knowing my hair was falling out. That said, every time I sneezed, I could imagine hair separating from my scalp, like a porcupine throwing quills. After feeling the shock and the relief, I was left feeling nervous about the coming transition from hair to scalp.

There was also, for me, some bizarre affirmation about my hair falling out as I was beginning my pilgrimages. I felt oddly connected to countless religious people through the ages and around the world who shaved some or all of their hair as a sign of a holy journey, ordination to religious orders, or taking monastic vows. It is customary for Muslim pilgrims traveling to Mecca to shave their heads. Buddhist monks shave not only their heads but their faces as well, continually keeping them shaven as a sign of their orders. Hindu practice includes the shaving of a child's head as a first haircut, sometimes leaving a tuft of hair at the crown. Monks in the Jain tradition don't shave the hair, they pull it all out. The ancient Celts shaved a crescent shape into the hair from ear to ear, while other Christian monastics sometimes shaved all but a thin ring of hair, and still others shaved a smallish circle just on the crown of the head.

"Taking the tonsure," shaving one's hair, was a sign of one's religious commitment. Suddenly it couldn't be more perfect that, as I packed up the car for my first pilgrimage, I was becoming bald. I could only hope to have a neat little circle of scalp on the top of my head by the time I drove down to Weston.

On my chemo day, I had picked up a pamphlet in the oncology waiting room about head coverings; I pulled it out of my "chemo day" bag and paged through it. In a relentlessly chipper tone, the pamphlet illustrated a dozen ways to tie a scarf on your head. At the end, it noted, "If scarves aren't your thing, perhaps you might like to try a turbine!"

Best. Typo. Ever.

Yes indeed, if I tire of the old scarf, I'll go for that classy "windmill on your head" look that's so fetching. Thanks for the fashion tip.

My pilgrimage packing list contained the usual summer camp items (sunscreen for my over-sensitive skin, bug spray to keep insect venom out of my blood, an extensive first aid kit), as well as bags of pharmaceuticals, piles of books, a few knitting projects, bottled water, and many bottles of Purell. This would be my first foray away from

Burlington, and I was worried that without a fully functioning immune system, I could pick up a bug from someone that would knock me on my back. Of course, I had that same concern in Burlington, but I lived within ten minutes of the hospital and a team of people who knew me. Now I would be stepping out into the world on my own, for the first time since the diagnosis. It was, to be honest, much scarier than I had thought it would be.

Weston Priory stretches out on its rural hilltop, a few miles north of trendy Weston, Vermont. Just as I remembered, gardens and buildings opened onto pastoral stretches of fields, barns, a courtyard, and the chapel, inviting in anyone who had found their way to it. I parked my car and went into the light-filled bookstore for my key and welcome information.

The women's guest house was back down the driveway a bit, so I headed that direction to find my room and get my belongings put away. I have always loved the cozy guest rooms in monasteries. Usually plain and tiny, they seem deeply restful to me. Sometimes the room includes a little sink as well, and in rare occasions, a private bathroom. However, sharing a bath doesn't bother me (and in Week 3 of the cycle, my bodily fluids were not at Hazmat levels), and there were several in our guest house to choose from. I saw that other rooms had been taken, but mine was tucked into a corner and had just enough room for a twin bed and a small desk and chair. Perfect.

After I'd hauled things in from the car and opened my window to catch the breeze, I hiked back up the road to the monastery, where it was almost time for Vespers. I took a seat in one of the chapel pews, near the back, and bowed my head. Here I was, making a start. Here I was on my first pilgrimage, feeling nervous and shy, wondering why I had thought this was a good idea, wondering why I'd left the safe enclosure of my apartment to knock up against all these strangers, and these monastic brothers who wouldn't remember me anyway. Silently, I cracked my frightened heart open and just let all the broken pieces lie exposed to the still chapel air, and for the first time I allowed myself to ask what was written on my heart. "Heal me, God. I don't want to die. Heal me, please."

The monks came in and began to sing, and I hummed along with them as I learned the song. Then the reader for the first lesson stood up, and read this passage from the prophet Amos:

> On that day, says the Lord GOD,
> I will make the sun go down at noon,
> and darken the earth in broad daylight.
> I will turn your feasts into mourning,
> and all your songs into lamentation;
> I will bring sackcloth on all loins,
> and baldness on every head;[7]

Yes, the reading went on, but I didn't hear any more. Of all the lines in the entire Bible, how did the first reading of my first pilgrimage turn out to speak of baldness, and in the very week that my hair was falling out? I blinked back tears and raised my face to the roof. "Thank you, God. Thank you."

My days at Weston Priory were remarkable in their sweetness. At supper on the first night, Brother David asked me when I had visited last, since I looked familiar. When I told him it had been thirty years almost, he cocked his head and smiled. "Ah! The Walk for Peace and Justice?" I was flummoxed. "Well, yes. Precisely." Perhaps for these brothers, as with God, thirty years was like the blink of an eye.

As I helped wash dishes after the deeply satisfying meal of soup and bread, he told me he knew two other people named "Cricket," but they were Spanish. Hmm, I'd never thought that I had international "sisters" who shared my name. We beamed at each other over the sink, and the thirty years since my last visit evaporated. The twenty-five-year-old me resurfaced, took my hand, and whispered in

---

7. Amos 8:9–10.

my ear. "Remember now? You have always loved it here." Ah, yes. I
had, indeed.

One of the intriguing aspects of a monastery has to do with the
daily schedule. A basic monastic tenet, at least in the Benedictine tradition with which I'm most familiar, is that every moment of the day
is equally of value, equally important in a life dedicated to praising
God. This understanding is meant to allow a radical freedom throughout the day, in which haste or perfectionism or clinging to one task
as being "more important" than another is released. If every moment
of the day is equal in value, then all of your tasks are equal. Washing
dishes after a meal is as holy as praying in the chapel, which is in turn
as important as working in the bookstore, weeding the garden, visiting with a guest, or folk-dancing in a field.

If you truly believe this, then when a bell rings to end a morning
work session and transition to chapel time, you can lay aside the task
at hand without being frustrated at the inability to finish it. Bells ring,
tasks change, and yet your day is never interrupted. It is all one fabric
woven of work, leisure, prayer, and sleep.

When I went to bed the first night, I had a familiar argument
with myself about whether I would set my alarm to go to Vigils at
6:00 am. As a rule, guests at monasteries are invited to attend all the
services, but are not required to attend any. Still, as a guest in someone's home, I generally try my best to participate fully (although I will
admit that years before, visiting the Cistercian Assumption Abbey in
Missouri, I had responded less cheerfully when my alarm went off
at 2:45 am for their 3:15 service). I am not an early-morning human.
Never have been. Monastics, though, rise early, greeting the day with
praise, and I did have sweet, fond memories of my former visits to
Weston, pulling on heavy, warm clothes for the frosty uphill walk to
the chapel in the predawn silence, opening the heavy chapel door
and feeling a rush of warmth that melted my frozen face, settling
into a seat, still half asleep, while the monks raised up their scratchy
morning voices in ever faithful song. It was intimate, and profound,

to huddle in the dark space, waiting for the first beams of sunlight to touch the windows.

Thus began an internal conversation about striking a balance on my pilgrimages, one that would keep tugging at me in the months to come. On the one hand, I wanted to steep myself in these communities, to challenge myself to live a holy and prayer-filled life while with each one. At the same time, I was nervous about my health and ability, and loathe to push my limits in case I found myself unable to recover my stamina or strength, once spent.

So should I get a really good night's sleep, or set the alarm clock for 5:15 am, so I'd have time to dress and hike up the hill to church? Feeling a little guilty, I set my clock for 7:00 am, and fell into a solid sleep.

But ah, at 5:15, one of the other guests came and pounded on the door next to mine, in a scene that was to be replayed every morning. "Pssst," came the loud, hoarse, whisper, "Elizabeth, Get up! You wanted to walk up to the church with me, right? Elizabeth? Wake up!" More pounding on the door.

I sighed and tried to pull a pillow over my head, as Elizabeth, whom I never saw during my entire visit, called back that she was going to sleep in. Her friend would have none of that, and continued pounding on her door. Our guest rooms shared an adjoining wall, so the pounding shook my bed as much as if the person had been banging on my headboard. For the next half hour of pounding and conversation, I debated going to my own door to ask the person in the hall to please stop, but the idea of sticking even a toe out into the cold room, while I was so warmly cocooned in my bed, made it seem an impossible task. Plus, I kept thinking that the "friend" would give up and go away. No such luck.

Well, maybe I could reframe this as a win/win situation. I got both the experience of praying in the predawn light (though I admit my prayer was an incoherent mishmash of "please go away, please shut up, please stop"), and then the ability to fall back to sleep finally, when the friend realized she was going to miss church if she didn't hustle herself up the steep driveway to the chapel.

Life in community. It's never simple.

The next day was the St. Benedict festival day, and it dawned bright and warm and dry. Perfect. Following breakfast, those of us who were staying onsite found chairs by the small lake, and watched as cars and people on foot made their way up the hill, toting picnics, coolers, and chairs. I had made two buddies among the many guests, one a teacher and the other a second-career doctor. Both were, like me, openly seeking more healing, more depth of relationships, more openness to the holy and numinous in their lives. We sat in the sunshine, alternately chatting, napping, and gazing out over the water and the beautiful vegetable gardens.

The main service was held in and in front of the large barn. With the front doors slid open, people arranged themselves on benches, and in lawn chairs, and on blankets, like an open-air rock concert. The brothers, resplendent in their Sunday robes and with many toting guitars, led a service that bridged tradition with playfulness, welcoming each one of us, meeting us where we were. Behind us in the fields, sheep bleated happily during both the songs and the silences. I stood in the sun with my new friends, as we sang together the words of the opening song, which turned out to be "We are on a pilgrimage. . . ."

Smiling, I realized I was no longer surprised by these resonances with my life.

At Weston Priory, you learn to expect them.

Chemo Round Two

Checking in for round two, I felt both prepared and hesitant. Round one hadn't been like anything that I'd expected. Would I continue to feel as well and strong as I did that morning, or would this and subsequent rounds begin to chip away at my sense of health and strength? Not infrequently, people would ask me how I felt and, when I said, "Surprisingly well," they responded with some version of, "Well, the effects are cumulative. You'll feel worse soon. . ."

Helpful? Not so much.

Why do people do this? How many times have I been in a gathering where someone announced she was newly pregnant, and within five minutes women were sharing horror stories of miscarriages, birth defects, or traumatic deliveries, while the recently joyful pregnant woman grew silent and ashen. One reason I didn't tell many people about my cancer was my desire not to talk about my, or other people's, cancers. It wasn't that I didn't care; I simply didn't have the strength to bear more worry than my own. Even my mother's face, behind her careful expression, still reflected the awfulness of the illness and death of her best friend Jessie years before from breast cancer. For many people, cancer wears the face of a loved one, now gone.

I also wanted to continue to be my "whole self" in these months. Well-meaning friends might think that every time they saw me, I would want to answer questions about my treatment and my health, but honestly I just wanted to keep on with my regular life. By not telling people about the cancer, I could laugh with friends over dinner about anything under the sun, and not fear that the conversation would turn to my health over and over and over again. I really didn't want to have illness and death suddenly be the front-and-center piece of my life. Cancer was one thing I was dealing with in my life, but it was not my whole life.

People also gave me "cancer books" with the best of intentions, thinking that I would be inspired by other people's journeys. Time and again, I would flip first to the author's bio to see if he or she was dead. If so, I put the book aside, and never touched it again. What are you thinking, people? I needed to keep my focus on being and staying alive. I didn't have the heart to read about someone else's "brave fight," only to hit that chapter in which the drugs stopped working or the cancer returned.

This is precisely where the work I was doing in therapy hit the road. If I believed almost everything on the internet I could find (*oh, right, I wasn't reading anything on there anymore, was I?*), then each round would indeed take a bigger bite out of me. If I expected to feel sicker each week, would that color the honest acceptance of where I found myself each day?

I was soaking up Buddhist teachings and writings, arguing and embracing and examining this radical and (for me) new way to walk through this time. I found these insights both affirming and challenging. Yes, you can *choose* how to experience the world, yes, you can *choose* to react or to respond. I didn't have to be a victim of this cancer. I could rely on my own basic goodness and trust my relationship with my body. Even though I had felt betrayed and shocked at the discovery of this cancer, healing was quietly seeping into that relationship, because I was learning to accept my life as being an OK place to be.

Chögyam Trungpa writes, "Often, when someone tells us not to be afraid, we think they're saying not to worry, that everything is going to be all right. Unconditional fearlessness, however, is simply based on being awake. Once you have command of the situation, fearlessness is unconditional because you are neither on the side of success nor on the side of failure. Success *and* failure are your journey." [8]

This is the pilgrim's path—not the need for everything to be perfect, but the deep desire to experience everything as it happens. To be alert to the bandit or the friend, without expectation or judgment. Here is a perfect foothold, here is the path through the forest, and here is the uncrossable river or the hungry wolf. They are all part of the journey. I was learning, imperfectly, not to label events or thoughts as "good" or "bad." I was discovering how to live my life with gentleness, curiosity, and vulnerability. Trungpa's phrase, to "have command of the situation," doesn't mean you are grasping to be in control of events beyond your power, but rather that you are fully present to that moment and whatever it holds. Our word "command" contains deep within it the alternative meaning, "to commit with strength." You commit to the situation you are in, not running from the scene because you are frightened. If you are sad, you feel the sadness. If you are angry, you feel the anger. You give yourself permission to be fully alive in the joy and junk of your honest life. Gently, lovingly, you commit to your life, and it is there that you find unconditional fearlessness.

Desperate myself to find this fearlessness, as if my life depended on it, I was doing my seated meditation, I was tearing through books

8. Chögyam Trungpa, *Smile at Fear: Awakening the True Heart of Bravery*, ed. Carolyn Rose Gimian (Boulder, Co: Shambhala Publications, 2010), 73.

day and night, I was spending hours in therapy asking, prodding, and often rejecting these ideas before coming back to embrace them. "What do you mean, 'don't react' to the news that I have cancer? Are you completely out of touch with reality? Of course it's bad news—what else could it be?" Gently, patiently, Max would explain it to me again. "Try to be curious. Try to scan your body and see what you are feeling. Hold there and explore that feeling. Touch and go. Don't run away."

Frequently I pushed back, sometimes incredulous, sometimes sad that it seemed beyond me, sometimes just furious with what I interpreted as his lack of compassion. "Screw this," I'd say. "It makes no sense." And Max would respond by telling me to get out of my head, stop worrying about sense and nonsense, and just breathe and try to be present in that moment.

Over and over again, I think this saved my life.

Thresholds—they are what I do. Without making a conscious decision, in situation after situation, I *wake up* and find myself in a doorway, on a threshold, shaking hands. After almost thirty years of being a parish priest, standing at doors and greeting people is how I'm wired, even when I have nothing to do with the event. I find myself frequently standing at doors welcoming people at concerts, gatherings, office parties, even once, embarrassingly, at a faculty party where I was a guest and had never met anyone there, including my host. Imagine my host's surprise when he came up the steps *of his own home* to find me, a total stranger, with my hands outstretched to him: "Hello, lovely evening, coats go in there, powder room—top of the stairs on the right. So glad you could come!"

So I guess it was no surprise that this was how I treated the oncology/hematology waiting room. There was something desperately sad about finding myself alone in that waiting room, after years of sitting with people in similar rooms. The first time I was directed into the windowless, small space, I looked around to see who my new people would be, and it was a true spectrum of humanity. Elderly couples silently clutching each other's hands, pale teenagers with a parent chattering away in denial, middle agers like myself with a parent or a child to keep them company. Some folks looked nervous but still relatively healthy, and others were wearing wigs or bravely sporting their bald heads. Nobody ever seemed to be sitting there alone.

When I arrived for any treatment, I would present myself at the check-in desk, where a smiling older fellow named Doug would wave me over to his cubby. We discovered we shared a fondness for show tunes, so each visit he would pick a show, and I would sing him a medley of my favorites as he checked me in. It became a moment in my day to look forward to, and he and I became good friends over those many months.

The idea of moving from check-in to the waiting area and sitting down, proclaiming my alone-ness to the world, was unthinkable. It felt like my private shame. Instead, I did what I do when I feel uncomfortable, and stood in the doorway of the waiting room, throughout the entire six months of my treatment. Because the department was not well marked, the first sign of a new patient was to see him or her wandering slowly down the hallway, reading the signage and peering into one room after another. As they approached, I'd give a cheery smile, "Looking for the oncology/hemotology lab? Waiting room?"

They'd show me their paperwork, or explain which doctor had sent them down, and I'd show them which department to check into and where. "That window is for the lab, just hand them the yellow sheet and they'll call you," or "See the line over there? If you stand in the line, when one of the admission folks is free they'll call you right in and get you all settled. The line moves pretty quickly—not to worry."

The self-appointed hostess of the waiting room, my default setting is so wired to be of service, especially at difficult times in people's lives, that it felt comfortable and safe for me to fall into my usual role. That way, I could forget for a moment here and there that I was also a *patient* in this oncology department. Standing at the door was my tiny rebellion of denial, like "Maybe I just work here, maybe I'm just finishing this shift in oncology, and then I'll wander down to the cafeteria to do something else. I don't actually have to be here. I can leave at any time."

It's not that I ever could forget for any long stretch of time that I had cancer, but sitting down in the waiting room to me felt like defeat. Give me a number and tuck me into a corner—that doesn't work for me. I'm used to making other people feel at home and comfortable, at weddings and at funerals, at social gatherings and at the altar on Christmas Eve. Acting like the Oncology Hostess helped me remain myself, in a situation that scared and galled me.

The worst part of that waiting room was the inventory of symptoms and side effects we had to fill out. I honor the fact that the staff needed to know details of each person's health, because as those poisonous drugs coursed through our bodies, all sorts of reactions and interactions took place and everyone's personal chemistry reacts differently to the cocktail of drugs they are given. Many of the side effects, uncomfortable, painful, or just distressing reactions, can be ameliorated by yet another drug, or by some other wisdom from the nurses—if they know precisely what your reactions are. Nevertheless, the inventory of side effects seemed to directly contradict my operating principle, which was to focus my mind and energy on feeling well. I was nervous that simply reading through all the side effects several times a week might cause my subconscious to create those very issues in my body. I know I am very susceptible to the power of suggestion.

At every check-in, two or three or more times a week, each patient is given the inventory, two sheets of horrors in tiny print, single-spaced, badly photocopied and slanted on the page. Across the top are the standard categories: no symptoms, mild symptoms, symptoms disrupting daily activities, major debilitating symptoms.

Every visit, even just for a blood draw, began with the ritual reading of symptoms: "Hmm. . . nausea? Pain upon urination? Mouth sores? Numbness in fingers and toes?" One after another, the Litany of Horrors continued. Symptoms that I'd never heard of and didn't want to imagine had to be considered and rated. "Esphogeal Ulcers? Anal Fissures? Erectile Dysfunction?" (Just for the record, I always checked off Erectile Dysfunction—I'd never had an erection. Might as well be honest, right?)

I believe that we find what we expect to find and we receive what we expect to receive. Just reading that list, in my opinion, increases anxiety and causes the mind to scan the body expecting to find problems and pain. When my toes became numb, I was actually excited finally to add something into the inventory, as if having side effects was a competition, and I had been falling behind.

I am not an unrealistic Pollyanna, but I fervently believe that our ways of thinking become habitual. *Looking* for bad news or problems does, inevitably, lead to *finding* those very things. Conversely, looking for good things leads to finding them. I actually created a "gratitude inventory" that I offered to the staff as a possible handout. My inventory contained questions like, "Name three things that you are thankful for today," and "What can you do to brighten someone else's life today?" Focusing my thoughts on a larger picture than my own pain, suffering, and illness reminded me daily how fortunate I was, and how precious every moment of my life was. As time wore on, I used the Litany of Horrors as a prayer list, knowing that some who read through the list were suffering deeply from these very issues. In my mind's eye, I paused at the reading of each symptom, and sent out a wave of love and healing to my companions on the path who were engulfed in pain and fear. I knew too well how fragile my equanimity and health were, and how quickly everything might change. This made each passing moment all the more precious, all the more a source of intense gratitude. "In this moment, I am okay. May comfort and healing be with those who are not okay in this moment. May they be free from suffering, and the causes of suffering."

I was prepared for round two of the chemo exactly three weeks later, but my blood work didn't look great. They wanted certain numbers to "bounce back," and mine were sluggish. My white blood cells were cowering in my veins, and the doctors don't like to hit you with another dose of chemo while you're down, so my chemo date was pushed forward several days. To remedy the sluggishness, I would now have to come into the infusion suite the day after each of my chemo treatments, to get a shot of Neulasta, which would stimulate the growth of healthy white blood cells.

Chemo round two finally came, and I went in alone. There were friends I could have called, but having gotten through the interminable first round with two supporters, I thought I'd do this round differently. Having friends and family sit with me was wonderful, but I worried about them, about how it looked to see me hooked up to bags of poison. So, this time, I just went on my own.

Most of the nurses knew my name by now, laughing with me as I sang a selection of tunes from *Brigadoon* while they accessed my chest port,[9] covered it with the sterile, see-through bandage, and left the IV line hanging through the buttons of my shirt. There was always the debate about whether to have a shot of Lidocaine before the sharp, thick end of the IV line needle was pushed through my chest. I had been all right not having the extra shot, but this time I accidentally looked over and saw the terrifying length of the port needle. Somehow in my mind, I had thought it would only be, well, skin deep. Say, a quarter of an inch. The one and only time I glanced over at it, it looked like it was four inches long and thick as my thumb, all of which was about to be buried into the tender place in my chest where the port

---

9. "Access" here is a euphemism for trying to distract you while hooking a monstrous needle through your chest into the port implanted under your skin.

had been stuffed under my skin. Oh Jesus, more drugs—yes, I'll take the Lidocaine shot, thank you very much. I'll take all the numbing you can give me. Sadly, it was too early for a martini. Wouldn't it be brilliant if hospitals had bars?

Hospitals do offer all sorts of services to cancer patients, mostly free of charge, ranging from support groups to cooking classes to stress management seminars. Local support networks in the area offered even more opportunities: free hiking and camping trips, fly-fishing classes, kayaking and canoeing events. Cancer is, strangely, your entry ticket into an entire parallel universe of activities, community, and wellness opportunities.

During my second round of chemo, there was a strolling massage therapist. Seriously. I watched as she went from one infusion cubby to the next, wondering if I had to flag her down. But no, she was quietly asking each patient if they would like a shoulder and scalp massage.

As her strong thumbs dug into my knotted-up shoulders, I know I moaned aloud. Oh my. I had missed this, missed having someone lay hands upon me and channel healing and kindness into my tightly clenched body. Living alone, how I missed just the simple act of being kindly touched. That healing went to deep places inside me, and I let down my guard and felt my muscles unwind. Sadly, I never again saw her in the infusion suite. I should have asked my oncology team to schedule my chemo around her volunteer schedule.

After the massage therapist that morning came a pet therapy team, an older woman with a standard poodle on a leash, proudly bearing a "Working Companion Dog" harness. The poodle and I shared some soulful looks as the handler chatted with the nurses.

Across from me, in a facing infusion chair, I watched a man about my age carry on with what seemed to be his workday, while hooked up to his chemo IV. He was on his phone most of the day, with his computer booted up on the tray table. He and the person on the phone were talking about clients and accounts, while he worked his way through a box of the locally famous Al's French fries.

Watching him, I wondered what it would have been like if I had gotten cancer while I had been working full-time. God knows I understood the desire to keep on going, not to slow down, to squeeze as much as possible from each day, to pass for normal. I'll never know what choices I might have made about working full-time or part-time or taking a medical leave, but I know that I was deeply grateful not to have to make them.

My priest pal Chris, who lived in another state, was fighting breast cancer at the same time I was in chemo. She was keeping up with her work, and my heart ached for her. Photos of her, tall and bald and determined behind her altar, reminded me how very deeply our vocations run in our hearts and brains. For me, so much of the priesthood is about sending energy outward to others, being in some way a conduit of sacred acceptance, forgiveness, and blessing. I felt selfish hoarding my energy all for myself, but I couldn't imagine having to share it, either. On the other hand, her parishioners routinely brought her homemade brownies laced with marijuana, so there was *that* bonus. (How would that even *happen*? "Good morning, Mother Chris—here's a little gift from my kitchen, containing a little something special from my garden." Seriously? I asked her to mail me some, before we both realized that would be, oh, a felony. I could just see the headlines: "Drug-Sniffing Dogs Uncover Unholy Package: Episcopal Priests Nabbed Trafficking Drugs Across State Lines." Sigh. Chris got to keep her brownies.)

As July wore on, I realized I'd be taking the fall off from graduate school, and made those arrangements. I wondered often about my classmates, all doing hospital internships that summer, and how they were getting along with the swallowing side of our speech-language work. I had been fascinated watching the barium swallow tests in our class, and wondered what it was like actually to perform the tests. Wryly, I thought ahead to the day when I could tell my classmates that I had indeed spent the summer in the hospital, only not as an SLP intern. Having stepped away from my job a year before to go to grad school, I was now stepping away from grad school to do chemo. I felt cut loose, in ways that were liberating and also frightening. Where was I? What was I doing? These months were just time-out-of-time, as though I'd hit the pause button on everything I'd been training for and everything I'd been working so hard on. In the span of that hour in the emergency department on May 20, my life had gone from "double speed" to hitting the slow-motion button and watching each moment clearly outlined in a frame of its own.

New Skete

Breeding dogs is an exceptionally tender-hearted vocation. While some monastic communities support themselves by brewing beer, making jelly, or baking bread, the Monks of New Skete are dog trainers and dog breeders. Breeding is a calling that both fills and breaks your heart, over and over again. It takes an enormous amount of courage, and faith, and resilience. I had purchased a book on dog training written by the Monks of New Skete when I got my first puppy and found their insights into all things canine touched a deeply spiritual place within me. I couldn't imagine a more perfect combination for a healing journey—prayer and dogs!

When I emailed the guest brother about pilgrimage time at New Skete, he said they had rooms for self-directed retreatants, meaning there wasn't a set retreat program but that people were welcome to come stay, join them for worship and meals, and even meet with a brother for spiritual direction if desired. I said I would be glad simply to have the time and space to be there on my own, and we scheduled a three-day visit.

From Burlington, New Skete was an easy two-and-a-half-hour trip. Or it is if you don't leave your directions at home on the kitchen counter. Basically, I only had to make one turn. After two hours southbound on Route 7, I would turn right through Arlington, Vermont, cross over into New York State, and voila, I'd be there.

At least, that was the theory. In practice, my GPS doesn't work in rural areas where there are no reliable phone or satellite signals. One gets used to these gaps in Vermont, hence the handwritten map and notes. However, I figured for a place as famous as they were, I could just find Cambridge, New York, and then follow signs to the well-known community (Not sure what I was thinking—big signs saying: "Monks and Puppies, three miles"?).

In the 1960s, as our country went through tumultuous times, religious orders were also rocked by change and new vision. Many monks, nuns, and clergy left their communities in order to engage with the world in new ways. Others sought to create new ways of living a monastic life by changing existing or founding new communities. New Skete was founded by twelve Byzantine-rite Franciscan monks, who left their order together to find a new way to live their vows as a community. The history on their website recounts the hard work and vision necessary to find a place to live, to make connections and alliances among their new neighbors, to continually reassess their choices to mirror their monastic vision, to build their monastery from scratch, and to try a variety of ways to make a living in their new rural community. Hard physical labor was balanced by the theological work of defining the community. Since their roots were in an Eastern expression of Christianity, they found themselves drawn to connect with the Orthodox Church of America.

Not long after the monks had settled in their current site, a small group of nuns left a women's Franciscan order called the Poor Clares, looking for a more contemporary monastic life for themselves. The women visited New Skete to learn about the community. They eventually purchased land nearby and in time became the Nuns of New Skete. Their website also mentioned a small community of married couples who had been attracted to the lifestyle and vision of the monks and had formed yet another expression of communal life as the Companions of New Skete. I was amazed by this ability of the community to keep extending welcome, to allow for new models of monastic expression to be considered and adopted. Clearly, these men were open to the very real direction of the Spirit, which continued to call them to live a life that was stable and yet continually renewed. I was eager to meet them.

I got myself good and lost in and around Cambridge. A lovely small town with shops, eateries, and several churches, Cambridge was friendly and welcoming. However, I didn't find any random signage pointing me toward New Skete. I suppose this was not a big surprise, since monasteries don't tend to be right on Main Street, but I had expected that I could still somehow find the place by trial and error. It was a beautiful summer's day, so I drove in leisurely loops out of town for several miles in each direction before turning back into the village again. Knowing they were an Orthodox monastery and having some experience of the Greek Orthodox church, I think I was scanning the rolling mountains for startling bright blue domes like ones seen in travel photos of the Greek islands. Strangely, as I drove through a gorgeous region of farms and fields and tiny towns, I saw nothing remotely resembling Santorini. Go figure.

I drove in pleasant circles for much of the early afternoon, but I did want to arrive with time to settle in before Vespers at 5:00 pm. So, looping back into the village, I found the post office, and went in to ask them where I'd find the monastery. Several people tried to direct me, in that charming fashion of local folk. "Oh, just turn right after the Townsend's farm." "See the stop sign? Well, don't turn there, but keep on going till you see the road past where the red barn used to be. . ." "If you see the high school, you've gone the wrong way. . ." Finally, one fellow walked out into the parking lot with me, and pointed. "OK, stay on this road. You'll cross two more intersections, but stay straight. Then in a couple miles, there's a sign on a pole where you turn right, though the sign sometimes falls down and gets propped at the base of the pole in the weeds, where you can't see it. . ."

That was as good as the directions were going to get, so off I went, not turning at the intersections, and finally only seeing the aforementioned sign when I did indeed pass a pole and noticed a board propped at the base. When I'd stopped farther ahead and turned the car around and come back, I saw that it actually did say "New Skete" on it. Victory was mine! I followed that road for a bit, and then another sign, thankfully still attached to a tree, pointed me left and up a steep dirt road toward the monastery.

At the top of the mountain, a circular drive showed off the exquisitely built church, replete with gleaming onion domes and distinctive orthodox crosses. The warm wooden structures with gilded spires were at once humble and awe-inspiring. The entrance was marked, and a sign asked visitors to ring a bell to summon someone. I rang, and was soon met by the guest brother, Gregory, who greeted me with warmth and good humor. In moments, I was tucked into a guest room and, having dropped my luggage inside, I scurried over to the main church to settle myself in for Vespers.

Stepping from the bright sunlight into the soft dimness of the church was like moving through a portal into a parallel universe. I halted just inside the doors and closed my eyes. The scent of incense hung in the still air. I breathed deeply, letting the sweet and mysterious residue of burnt offering fill my lungs, and through them, my entire body. The deep connection to our earliest ancestors struck me anew, as I imagined tens of thousands of years of humans offering gifts to the heavens by burning something aromatic and watching the smoke rise up to the clouds. If the scent pleases us, surely it must please the One who made us?

Orthodox worship is indeed a parallel universe to what we glibly call "real" life. I have always been drawn to the sheer, stunning sensuality of worship that refuses to sit tidily on a printed page, like my Episcopal liturgy. Icons gaze with infinite compassion in their eyes. The chanted service, at once simple and richly complex, carries through the air with no instruments to hide behind. The sign of the cross traced on forehead and chest was oriented long ago toward Constantinople and not Rome, a mirror image of the one I was familiar with from childhood. Sound, smell, sight—senses are overwhelmed in Orthodox worship. In a deliberate mastery, every detail is woven together to transport the human into a place apart, a place of holiness.

And so, perhaps *because* of the overpowering assault on my senses, maybe it was no surprise that, after I bent to kiss the icon by the door, after my eyes roamed in childlike wonder around the frieze of saints and holy men and women that surrounded the nave, after I selected a seat from the large, wooden chairs facing the iconostasis, and just after I noticed that the largest image in the space—an icon painted and gilded on the wall over the sanctuary—was Hagia Sophia ("Holy Wisdom"), my lifelong touchstone for God: after all of these moments, I experienced the most deeply inexplicable and mystical event of my life.

Here is what happened.

The church was dimly lit, since I was about twenty minutes early for Vespers.

I was alone. I settled into the roomy chair, placing my feet flat on the floor. Then I closed my eyes and settled into my breath.

I did not have an out-of-body experience, but rather I had whatever the opposite of that might be. I had a deeply *embodied* experience as my breath, laden with the hint of incense, dropped me down, down, down to my core.

I felt myself settling into the warm wood of the chair, actually being the chair, being the wood, being *living* wood. My breath moved through me like the breeze through tree branches, stirring, moving, but also centering. And then, deep within my feet I felt movement, a growing pressure and shifting sensation. The pressure grew in strength, a pushing of something against the inside of the soles of my feet, and then—I could imagine it almost as if I were watching it in a movie—I felt the bottoms of my feet open up and roots began to grow from the soles of my feet. Thick, snaking roots grew through my shoes and into, and then through, the carpet and the wooden floor. I sensed them stretching and growing down, down, down, until I felt them grasp at the very core of the earth. Then, they stopped and held.

And in my reverie, this all seemed normal. Startling, but not unnatural. A complete stranger in this place, surrounded by the watchful eyes of countless icons, I had rooted.

As I sat, breathing and wondering what this sign could mean, one of the monks came in and switched a few lights on. Behind me, in the sacristy/vesting room, I could hear a scuttle of feet and low voices as preparations for worship were made. The door to the church opened, and in came several smiling, silver-haired women. They tucked themselves into a tiny entry room, only to emerge in a moment in monastic robes. Carrying thick binders of music, they kissed the icon at the entrance and then made their way to seats in the center circle of chairs.

Slowly, monks filtered in from the vesting room and took seats in the circle.

Binders of music were set on stands, as each monk settled into a seat. Bells began to ring outside, but not the regular *dong, dong, dong* of a tolling bell, nor the odd, mathematically precise peal of British/Anglican change ringing. These bells were being jangled rhythmically, in clusters, a few more bells added onto each repetition. I was startled out of my rooted dream by their loudness, the bells raucous and strangely nonmusical. Following the bells, silence. The monks and nuns stood up, a note was quietly hummed, and the chant began.

Perhaps you are checking the back of this book right now, to see if it is cross-referenced under science fiction? Or maybe you have just googled my name, to see whether I survived this cancer only to fall victim to some sort of psychosis? I wondered myself whether some hallucinogenic drug had found its way into my pillbox.

I can't explain what happened in that church any better than I just have.

And if you think it was awkward to *read* about it, imagine my awkwardness when, at the end of this first worship service, in the first hour of my visit, I now had to introduce myself to these kind men and women who were my hosts, and decide whether or not to tell them that my feet had rooted themselves through the floor of their church.

Eh. Maybe better to wait. . . . [10]

As soon as the service was over, smiling monks and nuns came over to greet me, as I was the only visitor there. Warm handshakes, genuine smiles, and blessings for my retreat time tumbled around me. We walked out onto the front sidewalk together, and then the nuns clambered into two cars and drove off. The monks and I turned toward the refectory, and dinner.

If you have read the puppy or dog training books written by the community, then you have seen photographs of the monks at meals, with gorgeous German Shepherd dogs obediently lying on the floors near them. It was no surprise to have several dogs greet me as we lined up to say grace before we ate. The meal, like many monastic meals, was partly in silence. Often at a monastic meal, one monk reads aloud while the others eat in silence.[11] Here, quite practically, they listened to a book on tape so they could all eat together. My first evening, the "reading" was actually a recording of an interview with Eckhart Tolle on the public radio program *Fresh Air.* Again, this told me the community was open to all varieties of information, and that spiritual reading at meals was chosen with a broad-mindedness that one might not anticipate from a monastic community.

As soon as the tape was turned off, the monks began to quiz me about who I was and why I had come on retreat. Seated around one

---

10. As a matter of fact, it would be a year before I recounted this experience to one of the monks, in spiritual direction. Thank you, Chris, for not calling 911.
11. While at Weston Priory the month before, we had listened to a book about the history of the Mormon Church, which had been fascinating. Decades earlier, at a different monastery, I recall staring at my plate while a graphic book about the Holocaust was read aloud. Generally, the books are selected for their educational or edifying purposes, which might or might not make for comfortable mealtime listening.

long table, I felt like I was at a family reunion with a roomful of affectionate brothers, cousins, and uncles. They listed off all the Episcopal
clergy they knew, several of whom were also friends of mine. I nervously tucked strands of the wig behind my ears, having not told
them about the cancer yet, and gladly answered their questions.

One of the brothers was just back from a wedding in Portland,
Oregon, so there was much talk about the trip. Marc and I shared notes
about how tricky it is to choose and offer music in worship—it can be
too loud or too soft, or too fast for folks to understand the words, or
so slow you know you'll die of old age before the second verse is over.
Yet he and I agreed that music at its best invites and delights. Music,
for the monastic community, had to connect visitors with the monks
so that they were invited into worship together, instead of becoming
something for visitors to watch like a performance.

As trays of fresh fruit appeared for dessert, I had to "out" myself
as someone in the middle of chemo, and explain that I wasn't supposed to eat uncooked fruit or vegetables due to my compromised
immune system.[12] Gregory allowed as how there was an alternative
healthy dessert, and disappeared into the kitchen, re-emerging in
moments with a plate full of chocolate chip cookies. Who was I to
say no?

Meanwhile, I noticed that the puppy lying on the floor behind me
and Luke had slowly, imperceptibly, scooted himself along the floor
on his tummy, so as never to have looked like he was moving until he
came to rest between our feet, under the table. Luke, who had charge
of the pup, smiled indulgently as the little one leaned into him and
rested his head on Luke's foot. Raising large brown eyes, the puppy
clearly had tried his best to be obedient, but had needed a little support. Luke's eyes sparkled at the little guy, and he reached a hand
down to give the pup a little scratch around his ears.

---

12. Even organic produce was considered to be too risky to eat, too likely to
have had contact with fertilizers or chemicals.

One of my continual struggles with religion is the intersection of love and law. It infuriates me when religious laws or rules seem more important than love and compassion. As Luke comforted the puppy, I could see that here love outranked law, at least at dinner with the dogs. I reached down with a smile, and sank my fingers into the pup's thick fur. The little one gave up all pretense of obedience, and flopped over to offer his tummy for more of our attentions.

Since there was no programmed retreat, I knew I would have most of my time at New Skete to do with as I pleased. Of course there would be morning and evening prayers, and meals, but that still left most of the day free. It seemed to me I ought to try to spend some time each day involved in some sort of "Orthodox" pursuit, though I had no idea what that meant. I'm not artistically gifted, so trying to paint an icon was not going to fly. Searching around on the internet for other ideas within the tradition, I found directions for making a *komboskini*, an Orthodox prayer rope. Perfect. As someone who knits and spins, working with wool appealed to my desire to go deeper in some tactile way. I still remember with pleasure a relaxing evening, years ago, with the Episcopal sisters of St. Margaret's, during which I learned to tie nylon cord into the knots of an Anglican rosary.

Prayer beads, rosaries, *tesbih*, *malas*. Strung beads or knotted ropes have assisted people in saying their prayers in most traditions throughout history and around the world. Hinduism calls for 108 beads (or other numbers divisible by nine), Islam uses 99, while a Catholic rosary has 54 beads plus five, and Anglican prayer beads use 33. Shorter ropes or strings of beads are also common, with the understanding that you simply repeat the cycle of beads or knots until you reach whichever number was your goal.

Like chanting or meditating, repetitive prayer can be deeply centering. If there was a certain number of prayers to say, being able to count them off by feeling knots or beads move under your fingers helped keep the brain focused on prayer while not losing count. Simplest is to make knots in a length of leather, string, or rope. More complicated clusters of beads, bones, or seeds could signal a change in the prayer, or highlight when a special prayer was added. The Orthodox tradition had prayer ropes with a hundred knots in them. Fortunately, my directions for how to make one had not been left on the kitchen counter with my driving directions, so the next morning after breakfast, I broke out my directions and a long length of thick purple yarn, and went out to sit on a bench in the garden.

I hope you will do an internet search for *komboskini* and watch one of the videos demonstrating how to make one. The ones in Greek are especially entertaining. The bottom line is this: the special knot that is used in these ropes is supposed to contain seven interlocked crosses. I was the kind of kid who loved all of those cat's-cradle games with complex methods of twisting and capturing a length of string around the hands, but honestly the Orthodox knot had me slayed. It wasn't like putting a leader on your trout line, or a bowline in your tent fly. It was a complicated series of moves—looping yarn around different fingers only to unloop it a moment later, pulling the lines through gaps only to pull out previously tightened sections to undo them. I couldn't make head or tail of the knots, and after several hours had only an unknotted, tattered length of yarn to show for my efforts. And yet, it was the sort of mindful task that kept one very much in the present moment, since I realized I had been completely absorbed in the work for several hours without noticing the passage of time.

At lunch, Brother John introduced himself and, patting the seat next to his, asked me what I'd been up to so far that day. Sheepishly, I pulled out my length of yarn and showed him. "I've spent all morning trying to figure out how to tie an Orthodox prayer rope, but no luck. I had to pull it out every time, so I didn't even get one knot tied." John stared at me, and then flung his head back and roared with laughter. "Hey guys," he bellowed delightedly to the others around the table, "she's making a prayer rope—check it out. Good for you!" He thumped me on the back with the affectionate force of a grizzly bear, laughing till his eyes teared up.

Amused, John then launched into a story of a fellow who ties prayer ropes for the monastery gift shop. "Oh yes, he makes those hundred-knot, and sometimes the five-hundred-knot ropes. We have some in the shop now you should come look at." When I marveled that anyone could tie even one of the darned knots, much less make multiple ropes filled with hundreds of them, John continued. "Well, true. He is in prison, now that I think of it." Oh, swell. Hmm, my knitting group *was* called the Virtual Cellmates. Maybe I just needed to channel my Cellmates' collective superpowers to conquer the knot?

Oh, and I needed to use two different-colored pieces of yarn. It became clear that trying to keep track of which end went where wasn't working for me. One of the illustrations showed how to make the knot using yarns of different colors. By dinner time, I would have five knots to show John.

As lunch ended, Brother Stavros asked me if I'd like to say the mid-day service with him. We stepped together into the smaller church, their original Holy Transfiguration temple. More icons, carved wood, and the silky feeling in the air of decades of prayer gave the space a magnetic pull on my heart. Stavros explained that often he said the day's selection of psalms alone, but that it would be great to share the chanting. Honored, but feeling shy, I allowed as how I didn't know the Orthodox chants. He smiled. "No matter. Let's just alternate. You can use any psalm chant tone you like."

To a chant junkie like myself, this was bliss. He and I stood before the altar with a thick sheaf of the day's appointed psalms, our voices taking turns rising up in the warm midday air. Dust motes stirred in the slanting light, as though incense were rising from our breath. Once more, it was homecoming for me on levels I may never fully understand.

At dinner that night, I complimented the community on an intensely glorious tune they had chanted at Vespers. John laughed again. "Surely you heard the part where we messed up?" The men laughed good-naturedly at that, as we sat around the table again, this time with some other guests who had come that afternoon.

Conversations at New Skete could start anywhere, and go anywhere. That night, Christopher and I talked about the emerging uses of iPads when working with children with autism, which segued into a general discussion of the newly published Steve Jobs biography. Then, hearing that I was singing in the choir at the Episcopal cathedral in Burlington, the entire community told me a funny story about the time they had decided to visit the cathedral. Laughing and interrupting each other like best friends do, they finally got across the fact that, having found a door open, they had wandered in and up into the balcony to look at the art and architecture of the cathedral, but that somehow they tripped the burglar alarm. "Oh no," I laughed. "How on earth did you explain yourselves when someone came?"

"Oh no, we can't tell you what happened," Stavros laughed. "It would make you an accomplice!" By the end of the story, we were holding our sides, imagining this gaggle of Orthodox monks caught in the act of their non-crime. Once again, it felt more like a family reunion than a visit with strangers. I returned to my room for the second night having laughed so hard my smile muscles ached.

I had to leave on Saturday morning, missing Saturday night dinner with the nuns. Gregory remonstrated with me. "Are you *sure* you can't stay? We'll have cheesecake for dessert—it's not raw, so you can eat it."

Yes, the Nuns of New Skete make their living by baking cheesecakes. Later, when I told people how very much I'd enjoyed my pilgrimage, I would say, "Dogs and cheesecake. How could you get closer to heaven on earth than that?"

CHEMO ROUND THREE

C hemo round three was the giddiest of the rounds. Spirits were running high in the waiting room that morning— the usually quiet space rang with giggles and laughter. Blame our growing familiarity with the process and with one another, but we were more like ten-year-olds at a birthday party than cancer patients that morning.

A sizable group of us who had gotten friendly during the long chemo days pulled our chairs together and were discussing (maybe "grading" is more honest) the nurses and their levels of skill with accessing our ports. Of course, all of our nurses were wonderful, but the act of shoving that long curved needle into the subcutaneous ports did take some finesse. Most did it with little trouble, but occasionally someone would be filling in for a day and it was easy to tell that they were anxious about getting it right. Trust me, if they were anxious, we were too.

That morning, we were nicknaming the nurses by their styles: "the Ballerina," who danced around your chair getting everything set up just so before delicately easing the needle in; "the Waitress," who walked over in a no-nonsense way, slammed the needle in deftly, and moved on; "the Shrink," who always asked how you were, initiating a conversation before slipping the needle in during the distraction.

Each of the nurses had a style, and we enjoyed the range and unique-ness of each one, just as we were grateful for their friendship and care. For me, they had become like a room full of sisters, complimenting clothing choices, commenting on appearances, pausing to offer the Lidocaine or holding coffee while shirts were unbuttoned to expose the port site.

My parents were driving up that morning from Virginia, which may have been why I felt giddy. I hadn't seen them since my diag-nosis, and I was feeling protective of them and anxious about their worry for me. They hadn't arrived yet when I was shown into an exam room to catch up with the physician's assistant who was in charge of my case. He was the same fellow who had performed the bone marrow harvest on me, though I tried not to hold that against him. Looking at my chart, he asked me a barrage of questions about pos-sible side effects, none of which I was experiencing. "You are doing remarkably well," he told me, and I felt like I'd made the honor roll. Yay—I got an A+ in Chemo!

Just then, the door opened and in came my parents. How is it, no matter how old you are, when your parents walk into a room you feel as though you're about five years old? One minute, the PA and I were colleagues, chatting about the cancer, and the next minute my parents were asking questions about me and I just sat on the exam table listen-ing. Even after all the information the PA gave them about my cancer and the very high five-year survival rate, and his confidence that they had the right treatment plan in place, my parents were still anxious. I'll never forget my dad leaning forward with tears in his eyes, saying, "But Doc, can you save her?" My heart broke in two. Scenes from *Love Story* and every other tragic movie I'd ever seen ran through my head. The PA reached forward to lay a hand on Dad's arm. "Sir, we're doing our best. She should be just fine." Dad was so relieved, he had to step outside for a cigarette and, I imagine, a bit of a private cry.

My pal Dorothy also came to visit the infusion suite that morn-ing. After I was settled into that morning's cubicle, and my drugs were running, in she came with treats and books and her usual light-filled smile. Dad and Mom had wandered off to find the cafeteria and some lunch, so Dorothy and I had time to yammer, and catch up, and read through the palindromes in a book she'd brought. Our favorite was, "An era came—Macarena." For some reason, that made us laugh uncontrollably.

The cancer, once again, was put into perspective, as I realized that it was giving me the opportunity to make time in my life for my most beloved friends. While working, there wasn't time enough, but now I could have a whole morning with Dorothy, just enjoying her company. It was a pure gift.

Nevertheless, the Benadryl they gave me to stop allergic reactions took its toll, and when she saw me getting sleepy, Dorothy hugged me and headed out. Mom and Dad checked in and saw how zoned I was, so they headed back to their hotel, where I promised to meet them when I was done. It was a beautiful August day, and Dad was eager to sit by the outdoor pool with his new book. Mom was relieved to see that I was feeling fine and was looking forward to a few days to catch up on all the medical details.

Mom had recently announced to us three kids that she had been accepted into medical school. We were surprised, since she was in her early seventies, although she had been pre-med in college. Having left this news to dangle for a little while, she continued on to explain that she had filled out the paperwork for her body to be donated to science, and that, although she was in no hurry, she was excited to think that one day she would find her way back into a first-year anatomy class, as the cadaver. Only in my family would this be greeted with whoops of congratulations, as Mom's dreams of going to medical school were finally going to be realized—even if as a corpse—after having been put on a back burner in the late 1950s when she had married and started a family.

The chemo having run its course, I was free to enjoy their visit and show them some of my new favorite haunts around town. We had three days to visit and then I was off to Maine for my first taste of vacation since starting treatment.

Steve, who managed the retreat and conference center where I lived, had become a good buddy, and had been a rock for me during my diagnosis and treatment. Knowing there was someone nearby who would notice if I passed out or never left my apartment was a real comfort to me. Living alone while fighting cancer was much more frightening than I could admit, even to myself. Early on, when the doctor explained that the massive doses of prednisone I'd be given could, in "some people," cause psychotic episodes of behavior, I was alarmed. What were those like and how would I know if I'd had one? The doctor had said, totally seriously, that generally the person having the episode wouldn't notice but that people around him or her would be the ones to call 911.

Oh great. Steve reassured me that if he came in on a Monday morning and I was throwing furniture out of my second-floor window, or out in the woods howling at the sky, he would take charge of the situation. Laughing, he finished up, "What are friends for?" As silly as the scenarios were that we imagined, it was still a deep relief to know somebody had my back.

The weekend after chemo round three, I had the honor and privilege to travel to the Maine coast, to perform Steve's son's wedding. Our friendship, and my availability, made this arrangement easy, and when I met the bride- and groom-to-be, I was delighted. You don't always bond immediately with a couple that you're marrying, but these two were the best. I was thrilled to be a part of their weekend.

I didn't know, when Tom and I showed up for the wedding, who might or might not know about my cancer. The beauty of it was that I could slap on the wig, brighten my face up with a tad of makeup, and just keep on trucking. Flash forward to the rehearsal dinner night, where we found ourselves at a yacht club enjoying one of the best parties imaginable. Lobster, a great group of young people, fun folks our own age—it was a dream dinner, even as high winds and some spitting rain added more than enough Maine atmosphere to the evening.

Steve and I stepped out onto the pier to catch up. The greatest gift of the priesthood is being in the center of families during the pivotal moments of life. Births and baptisms, weddings, even funerals—these are events when families test their mettle. Some families lift up their wounds and brokenness in these times, making the journey or transition painful and hard. Some families, like Steve's, weave all of their history into the moment, bringing out the best not only in themselves but in the folks gathered around them.

As Steve and I stood on the pier with our drinks, I struggled to find a way to say how touched I was, how much it meant to me to share in their joy. But instead, a great gust of wind off the water shifted toward us. I felt it catch at my hair, and start to lift it off. I knew my wig heading out to sea would *definitely* put a damper on my weekend. Clapping my hand on my head, I looked up at Steve, laughing, and said, "Whoops, almost lost my head there. I'd better step back into the tent." He grinned and followed me back to the warmth and laughter of the party.

After the wedding festivities, Tom and I headed south along the coast to visit with our good friend Alan. We had gotten to know him and his wife, Carol, when he had been interim pastor at a Baptist church near us in New Hampshire. Now he was serving a parish on the Maine coast, and we were excited to visit for a day or two.

Alan was a professional musician as well as a pastor, and his church was hosting an open mic night that evening. Neither Tom nor I have ever been fainting wallflowers when given an invitation, so we instantly agreed to perform that night, still high on the love fumes from the wedding. I hadn't done anything like this since my days as a singing cocktail waitress in New Jersey, some thirty years earlier.

As I stood at the mic that night, in this lovely church on the coast of Maine, belting out "Funny Valentine" to a room full of strangers, I thought, "Huh. Nobody tells you that cancer can be like *this*. Cancer is getting this chance to be with friends, to take risks, to stand in front of a room singing my heart out like I haven't done in decades. Cancer is giving me this opportunity to say *yes* to my life, over and over again."

Saying *yes*. Cancer is that time. I could say yes to everything. How could I let a single moment slip through my fingers untasted, unfondled, unloved? Yes to the singing, to the perfect notes and the off notes, to the laughter and the tears and the connections with strangers and friends. I felt that weekend like a solar love panel, absorbing goodness from others, and storing it for less sunny days on the journey.

Karma Triyana Dharmachakra

Meditation has been misrepresented in the Western world. The term alone causes many people to get discouraged. Their understanding of meditation is that they must do it in a completely isolated place, under a tree or in a cave, and starve to death. They think that to meditate means to give up everything: family, house, possessions, wealth. With that conception in mind, the term meditation simply scares the wits out of them. But it is not true. Meditation does not mean that you have to give up everything. The method to unfold wisdom is practicing, and integrating the practice into our daily or worldly activity. That is meditation. Then slowly and gradually our spiritual strength and wisdom develops.

—from the website for Karma Triyana Dharmachakra,
kagyu.org

You, yourself, as much as anybody else in the entire universe, deserve your love and affection.

—The Buddha

As the time came for me to leave on each pilgrimage, I would find myself thinking, "This one will be the hardest. This will be the really intense one." This time, I honestly *knew* that Karma Triyana Dharmachakra would be the most challenging, as I had only visited Western Buddhist sites and communities. My sense was that visiting this Tibetan Buddhist monastery would be like visiting a foreign country. No matter how many guidebooks you've read, in the end you realize that nothing could have prepared you except the desire to let go of all your expectations.

Nevertheless, I obsessed over their website before I went. It offered a fascinating treasure trove of information, especially the details I most craved in order to prepare myself: etiquette directions. Leave your shoes outside, sit still on your cushion, be prepared for the teaching to be lengthy. Never stick your feet straight out in front of you. Treat each level of holy person with extreme respect, according to his title: *lama, rinpoche, tulku*. Terrified that I might inadvertently offend someone, I scoured the website, and saw the careful instructions about how to bow to this one or prostrate yourself to that one to show deference. I wondered how on earth I would know who was at what level. Many of the directions spoke of how to show respect if, for example, meeting or passing one of the teachers in the hall. I vowed to stay out of the hallways as much as possible.

KTD is the North American seat of the Karmapa, who is described as an "enlightened being . . . an embodiment of compassion." More than a teacher or respected elder, the man is considered a deity.

I was completely entranced, and entirely terrified.

I had signed up for a weekend class called "The Heart Sutra and Nothingness." Because my tumor was the same size as my heart, and lodged just a little above and beside it, I spent considerable energy meditating on my heart and sending it healing vibes. Nevertheless, trying to read the Heart Sutra in advance only helped me realize that this teaching was all new, and would be challenging:

Thus, in the state of emptiness, there is no form, feeling, thought, will, nor consciousness. . . it cannot be visualized or conceived. In emptiness there is no ignorance nor cessation of ignorance; neither senility nor death, nor the end of old age and death. The emptiness is no suffering, nor cause for suffering, nor end of suffering, nor a path. Nor is it the realization of wisdom, nor is it the negation of realization.[13]

In the back of my mind, I could hear the words of "Imagine" being sung by John Lennon. In this place, I would meet with many things, and with nothing. I was ready, I thought, to enter into this place of nothingness.

It was bright and sunny the day I drove to Woodstock, New York. Traffic was light, and I was eager to arrive as early as possible, to get settled in before the course started. The real trek to KTD begins as you turn off the main road through town to follow a meandering road to *another* road that leads impossibly up to the sky. I drive around and over mountains all the time, but I was a little freaked out at how the road kept going up, up, up—two and a half miles of nonstop ascent.

At the top of the mountain was the shrine. Tibetan prayer flags flapped tautly in the strong wind, blowing the blessings of the Buddha out and across the entire world. I fought the car door open and the cold air hit me. Down in the valley it had been a nice day, but up here it was blowing a gale. Grabbing my backpack, I looked for the office.

The buildings seemed oddly deserted. They were massive, with gleaming white facades intricately decorated. I stood in the gale force wind staring up at them, unable to find any signage or any people. I was nervous about going into the buildings (hallways, you know) and none of them were marked. I do know that religious communities often have entire wings or buildings that are not open to the public,

---

13. Anonymous, "Translation: Longer Heart Sutra," last updated June 14, 2016, https://en.wikisource.org/wiki/Translation:The_Longer_Heart_Sutra.

and I cringed at the thought of making some faux pas, stumbling into a building that was off limits.

Finally, I found a door ajar and wandered in. Pretty deserted. On my third nervous circuit of the whole first floor of the building, I heard typing behind a door that I'd just passed. I eased it open, and there was a young woman quietly working away. She greeted me with infinite kindness, inquired about my drive and my health, and handed me the key to my room and a map of how to find it.

Back into the (thankfully) deserted, crisscrossing hallways I went, until finally I found my room on another level, far at the end of a dimly lit hallway.

As it turned out, my room was huge, bright and airy, though they clearly hadn't yet turned the heat up for the event. No matter, as I had come early to get settled in. My map showed me where the bookstore was, so I wandered over to check it out, before going to the shrine room for the optional meditation hour.

There were a few people seated on scattered cushions in the shrine room when I entered. By now I had learned a few ways to bow and show my respect as I stepped into the large open room; I paused to bow to the shrine[14] before really looking up and around.

I felt like a Quaker at the Vatican. Never before had I seen a level of decoration to rival this, and I've visited holy shrines and sites throughout Europe and Canada. The front of the room was almost blinding in reflections and colors. The brightest reds of hanging fabric and paint reflected off shining gold bowls of water laid in perfect lines of devotion around the large gold Buddha in the center. There were

---

14. A colleague of mine asked if I ever felt duplicitous, bowing to shrines in non-Christian temples. The question never once occurred to me. As a guest in another person's worship space or monastic guest room, it felt only natural to me to honor the prophets of that tradition. I understand this can be a sensitive topic for some, but bathing my spirit in the sacred ways of many traditions was healing, and holy, for me.

flowers and other offerings piled around the bowls, almost spilling off of the altar in chaotic abundance.

Cushions for meditation and the evening program were neatly lined up throughout the space. I made my way into the center and snagged a mat that gave me a good view of the raised platform in front of the shrine, where our guest speaker would be. I had seen a photo of him, and he was an elderly man, a *lama*, meaning a highly respected teacher of the Dharma. I tried to remember just how to bow to him, if I met him in the hallway. There was also a lot of information on the etiquette site about offering a white silk scarf to a teacher, and then bowing to have the teacher place the scarf back around your neck. I honestly didn't know whether I was meant to have such scarves with me to offer, or if that was only for more formal, one-on-one teaching situations. In any event, I had gotten my excitement up to a fevered pitch by this point. Or could it be that after the long drive in the hot sun, skipping dinner, possible dehydration, and my own nervousness, I actually *was* a little feverish?

A bell was rung for meditation and I sank gratefully into a place of deep inner silence. Daily meditation was becoming a reliable companion and I felt more and more comfortable in these lengthy sittings, although my right leg did have a tendency to fall asleep. No matter. I was able to "dim down" the world around me and focus on my breath.

Forty-five minutes later, the bell was rung again, and I felt myself slowly resurface. Careful not to stretch my legs straight out in front of me, I tucked them momentarily to the side, and let the blood circulate a little more through them. It was only at this point that I realized that the person who had settled onto the cushion next to me had two laptops arranged on a cushion in front of him, and he was wearing some sort of headset, with a mic curved in front of his mouth. I tried not to stare, but as I rearranged my legs and waited excitedly for my first glimpse of this holy teacher, the fact that a full array of computer dings and an incessant barrage of typing noises were rising from the *zabuton* two feet to my right seemed shockingly disrespectful. But again, I was a guest here and not sure of their customs. "Unhook from this, Cricket," I reminded myself. "You're not in charge. You don't have to fix anything."

One of the evening's guides welcomed us, and explained that while we waited for everyone to gather, we would chant together for a time. The chant, *Om Mani Peme Hung* (Tibetan version of the Sanskrit *Om Mani Padme Hum*) was deeply intoned for us and we fell into it like a river on a summer day. The pull of the words and tone were inexorable, irresistible to me. Chanting has been a powerful tool for me in many languages and contexts throughout my life, and so even in this unknown setting, chant felt like the warm hug of a good friend. Repetition, deep rhythmic breathing, the feeling of the words washing over and through me, an alliance of breath with body and voice and mind—this was why I was here. I felt the space between and behind my eyes loosen and soften, as the waves of sound became my entire world and carried me on their back.

You might be curious, as I was, about what these words "mean." Ah. Everything? Nothing? Even asking the question shows how we long to make sense of the world, in lieu of simply experiencing it. You can read a great deal about what the words may or may not point to, but one of the most interesting things about the chant (to me, at least) is simply the six syllables, which point to other significant groupings of six that can be found in the tradition. It is said that all the teachings of the Buddha are contained in this chant. One website says that chanting the mantra, or spinning a prayer wheel with it written on it, or even just looking at the chant in written form, all invoke "the powerful benevolent attention and blessings of Chenrezig, the embodiment of compassion."[15] Well, if there was anything my entire chemo pilgrimage was about at its very core, it was benevolence, blessing, and compassion, toward myself and toward all others. I chanted until

15. "Om Mani Padme Hum: The Meaning of the Mantra in Tibetan Buddhism," http://dharma-haven.org/tibetan/meaning-of-om-mani-padme-hung.htm.

it felt as though the top of my head was open to the sky and sunlight was pouring into the chambers of my heart.

A rustle of cushions, beginning at the front of the room, signaled the arrival of the teacher. Quickly, we all got to our feet, as a short parade of important-looking men formally entered the room, followed by a tiny man with an impish smile to whom everyone immediately bowed low. There was much understated fussing about cushions and glasses of water; the elderly man found his seat and watched, still gently smiling, as things were arranged in front of him, ostensibly for his comfort during the evening's teaching.

Then a microphone was produced and an assisting teacher stood to welcome what was now quite a full room of people. He spoke many words of respect and thanks to the teacher, who bowed back with the sweetest of smiles to everyone and everything around him. There truly was something magnetic about this man, which could be felt, I was sure, to the farthest corners of the room, or maybe even the earth.

The translator reminded us that the teaching would be given in Tibetan, but that he would be translating into English for us. The teaching was also going to be translated and simultaneously broadcast in China, which seemed pretty impressive to me. With all the formalities out of the way, everyone settled onto a cushion, and the teacher began.

I would like to give you a brief synopsis of the teaching, but alas, it was lost to me. As the teacher began to speak into his microphone, the translator would listen intently and then speak the English into another microphone for us. Hardly had the first sentence in English been uttered than the fellow on the cushion to my right began to repeat everything in Chinese, into his headset. Oh no—he was the one simultaneously translating the lecture.

My time in the communication science/audiology department at the University of Vermont had taught me much about listening and learning and teaching. One gem was that if you really want to get someone's attention, or perhaps teach a child who is having trouble listening, the best thing you can do is speak into the right ear, which will take your message straight to the left side of the brain, where the major language centers are. Something as simple as this, saving the message the extra trip from one hemisphere of the brain to the other, can aid in better comprehension.

However, as I experienced that evening, it is also much harder to ignore a message being sent straight into your right ear. Honestly, I had no idea what to do. I knew standing or moving during the teaching was considered unspeakably rude. I assumed slamming one hand over my right ear would be similarly disrespectful. But even though English words were flying in the air around me, so were Tibetan words, and all of them seemed mostly drowned out by Chinese. I felt the bubble of anticipation that had been building inside of me all week slowly deflate and, instead of taking in the message that this holy man had brought us, I focused on my breath and my seated posture for the next several hours. Oh, and I vowed to sit in a distant corner the next day.

At last, we stood again as the teacher, still beaming, was led out. Those of us staying over had been given instruction to meet at the front of the shrine room following the teaching, to assist with various chores. These acts of simple service as a guest draw you into the community and give you an opportunity to show gratitude, and I shyly waited for the young man in charge of my service to give me a job. I was to empty and dry all of the glistening water offering bowls, resetting them on the altar for morning.

After more than twenty-five years as a priest, touching gem-encrusted chalices, gold patens, and intricately covered ciboria is as natural to me as picking something up from my own dinner table. But these large, heavy golden bowls of water had me in awe. I walked each one, singly, to the place where my guide had shown me to pour out the water, and then dried each one lovingly before returning it to the altar. In my memory, there were dozens and dozens of these bowls, although in reality there were perhaps only twenty. But at the end of a long day, plus the two and a half hours of seated teaching, the night seemed as though it would never end. By the time I wandered back toward my room, I was fully done in.

Although I would not have admitted it at the time, I think I was not as strong as I was professing to be, and that the chemo had started to take its toll on my body. After my quick personal ablutions, I fell aching into my bed as though I had hiked Everest, and felt every muscle in my body uncoil for sleep.

But, damn, it was cold. Not just "turn the heat down for bed-time" chilly, but *cold*. Like "sleeping outside in the winter" freezing. Mentally and physically shot, I dragged myself out of bed to see if the window was open. Nope. Okay then. I turned on the light again to find a thermostat, which clearly I'd forgotten to notice earlier. Nope. Maybe a small radiator along the wall that needed its valve turned on? Nope. Huh. I went into my little bathroom, thinking the con-trols might be in there. Nope. Let's check the hallway outside my bedroom? Nope. Slowly, my foggy brain realized the truth. There was no heat.

By now, padding about in my pj's and bare feet, I had only gotten colder. My teeth were beginning to chatter loudly against each other. Opening my suitcase, I realized I had packed only summer clothing and one thin fleece pullover. Methodically, I put on every piece of clothing I'd brought, and then I pulled all of the covers loose on the bed so I could lie down on one corner of them and roll up, like a bur-rito. Thus clad and wrapped, I wheedled my way back to standing, and then tilted myself sideways to fall over onto the center of the bed. My exertions had created a little heat, but soon I was just as cold as I had been before all of this, plus I'd forgotten to turn off the light. Like Houdini, I slid first one foot and then the other out of the bottom of my blanket roll, and hopped over to the light switch. My arms were trapped against my sides in the burrito blanket, so I knocked at the switch with my forehead until I hit it just right. Then I shuffled back and fell onto the bed a second time.

No dice. I cursed myself for not thinking to bring a sleeping bag along, or more clothing, or warm socks. Just the thought of my thick SmartWool knee-highs brought stinging tears of longing to my eyes, and some of the day's tension dissolved into weeping. After perhaps three-quarters of an hour, I had the idea to run hot water in the bathroom, and then perhaps with the door closed I could sleep in the hot steamy mist on the bathroom floor. Fighting my feet back out, I hopped into the bathroom. Nope. No hot water.

You know how it is when you aren't at your best and nothing is making sense? I lay in the dark, weeping gently and wondering if this was simply a reminder to the guests not to cling to worldly comforts. "Ah! That must be it," I thought to myself. "This is an opportunity for me to let go of my need to feel warm, my desire to be comfortable. . . ." This desire to embrace my discomfort vied in my head with the strong desire to go sleep in my car, with the heated seats turned up to maximum. Tears again poured down my cheeks as I fantasized about those seats. But no, in order for them to heat up, the car would have to be running all night. That wasn't happening.

Deep in the night, I began fantasizing about morning. The sun. Maybe they turned the hot water on in the morning for folks to get showered and ready for the day. And there would be coffee, of course, and very likely a bowl of hot oatmeal or something similar. Having skipped dinner earlier in the evening, I became fixated on breakfast. Perhaps hours went by as I imagined the coffee, in a thick mug, held close to my face and warming my cheeks.

The truth is, I have no idea if it was actually that cold, or if the chemo had just messed up my inner thermostat. I am someone who always runs cold, and not even my fifties had brought me the longed-for flashes of heat that so many of my friends experienced. God, how quickly I would have sold my soul to Satan for a hot flash that night. By morning, I could barely walk. I have had enough bouts with frostbite that my feet turn an alarming yellowish-white when they get chilled. That morning, with no socks, they looked like I'd painted them with highlighter. The water in the bathroom still didn't warm up, and I had to take off a layer or two of clothing, since wearing everything I'd brought seemed a bit bizarre, even for fashion-challenged me.

In the dining room, we guests stood in silence while a staff member opened the windows and doors of the room to air it out. I winced inwardly, dying to ask one of the others how the night had gone for him or her. Had I read the dorm map wrong? Maybe I was in the wrong building? Maybe I was on the wrong floor? Just then, the staff person lifted a giant conch shell to his lips and blew a rich, deep tone into the courtyard. Like the sounding of the *shofar*, the conch shell spoke of an ancient tradition that resonated deep inside my body. It was the sound of hope, the sound of breakfast.

The coffee was everything I'd dreamed of. Shockingly hot, I simply smelled it for the first five minutes, taking tiny sips from the side of my mug, and letting the heat sit on my tongue. I resisted the temptation to pour some into a bowl and put my feet in it, but only just barely. Stumbling a bit, I lined up at the buffet, and saw oatmeal. Again, my heart leapt. I could do this. I was strong and I would get past last night, and make a success of this visit.

The oatmeal was cold. So cold. I stared into my bowl, and tears again began spilling down my cheeks, unbidden and unstoppable. I stared at the chilly grains, resentful and angry, as though my best friend had betrayed me. The grains stared back, their tiny oat faces bland and unmoved by my tears. Holy crap, I was starting to unhinge completely. I turned back to my coffee mug and admitted to myself that I wasn't just cold, I was desperately unwell. At last, I could see how my final interior retaining wall had crumbled, and I was in emotional freefall.

Forty-five minutes later, I was in tears again, but this time they were tears of gratitude. Nestled into a sunny booth at the Phoenicia Diner, I was watching as the waitress thumped down a breakfast in front of me that might easily have fed a family of four, should any family of four want to eat an exotic breakfast of duck confit and grits.

Feeling the tingling pain of my feet warming up, and breathing in the glory that was my breakfast, I tried to shake off the embarrassment and shame I felt for grabbing my bag and sneaking out of the monastery. Was I honestly going to fail one of my pilgrimages?

Too much food and almost enough coffee later, I had made peace with my soul. I had not noticed how fragile my body had become. Skipping meals, not being able to keep myself warm, emotional fragility. The time had come to pay better attention and take better care of myself. The time had come for me to put into practice the self-compassion and love that I'd been reading so much about. The monastery and I had not failed each other, but our timing had been off. As I pointed my car north again on the New York Thruway, I reached out and clicked the heater on my feet up another notch.

Ah, life is sweet, and I was, after all, taking home the powerful lesson I had most needed to learn. Every day we are given fresh opportunities to show ourselves infinite compassion and tenderness. Some days, that just might mean a change of plans, and breakfast in a diner.

CHEMO ROUND FOUR

To be fully alive, fully human, and completely awake is to be continually thrown out of the nest.[16]

—Pema Chödrön

Three down, three to go. Past the halfway point. *I've got this.*

Coming in for round four was wonderful. To think, I was on the downhill slope. The PET scan results would be back, and the doctors would be pleased, and I would be counting down the second half of the treatment timeline. I was bubbly and jubilant.

And yet, when I checked in, something did not seem quite right. Instead of heading back into the infusion suite, I was tucked into one of those bland consulting rooms. There seemed to be a lot of folks milling around outside the door. My nurse popped in to say that the doctors wanted to talk to me about the results. She subtly rolled her eyes at this. Together, we had formed a team, and we shared a little of an "us against them" camaraderie. This began when my doctor had, before round one, told me that no alcohol was allowed during chemo,

---

16. Pema Chödrön, *When Things Fall Apart: Heart Advice for Difficult Times* (Boston: Shambhala, [1996] 2005), 88.

since I'd have enough chemicals in my system already. After he left the room, she said quietly, "It's really about how you feel, and what helps you feel better. If a glass of wine or a beer helps you chill in the evening, it's not going to hurt anything." So, with her refreshing permission to trust myself, we were buds.

The doctor and the PA came in with the PET scan results. I thought the scan looked amazing. Where there had been a glowing, fist-sized mass above my heart, there was only darkness. If you squinted, you could see a tiny, glowing edge on one section of the tumor, what the techs called "FDG uptake," meaning something in there was still eating, still living. But it was so tiny, and we were only halfway through, I thought, so what was the big deal?

Well, nobody really said this to me, but it became clear that they had expected the entire tumor to be quite dead by now. That tiny, almost invisible line should not have been there. And, for scientists, that small shimmer was a large problem.

"We're recommending you change now to the clinical trial protocol. The department is on the phone to your insurance, and we hope they'll agree to cover it. They may cover the chemotherapy but not the new mobile pump, in which case you'll need to be admitted as an inpatient to receive your infusions unless you can pay for the pump out of pocket. Oh, and instead of a one-day treatment, this takes five days. You'll come into the clinic every day now."

I felt like a knight in a jousting circuit. Fully armored and running full steam ahead that morning, I suddenly was being whacked from all directions, each successive piece of information denting my armor and knocking me off balance. Change chemo regimens—*whack*; insurance arguments—*whack*; in-patient treatment—*whack*; five chemo days—*whack*. And subtly, underneath all of this news, was the really scary truth: they were not pleased. The cancer wasn't responding right. I might not have a curable strain of this thing. Maybe I was going to die. *Whack, whack, whack.*

For the first time since round one, I was really scared. Kristen murmured that they might be overreacting a tad, but it was too late. I was held in the consult room while calls were made to my insurance, and while the doctors scuttled over to radiology to have an expert look over the scans again with them.

I sat and waited. This was another round when I didn't have anyone with me, and suddenly I deeply regretted my cavalier attitude. Swinging in here this morning so cocky about my minimal side effects, my fifteen-mile bike rides along the lake, my kayaking. It had all been in vain, because the chemo wasn't working. A whirlpool of doubt and despair caught me, and spun me down, down, down.

The physician's assistant stepped back in with an update: they'd reached the insurance company, and the new protocol *and* the pump would be covered. However, it was so late in the morning that they might have to wait until the next day to start me, and that would mean checking me into the hospital as an inpatient on Friday night, since the weekday clinic wouldn't be open to monitor my fifth day of treatment. He said he'd be back when they knew.

They were able to get me hooked up that day.

This time, day one of chemo would be a longer day as they dripped some of the new cocktail into my veins while I was at the hospital. Then the remaining chemo cocktail would be split into four IV bags. Each successive day of the week, I would return to the clinic to get the new bag attached to a pump device that I would carry with me in a navy blue Cordura messenger bag.

But wait, that's not all—the surprises just kept coming.

One of the lab techs came over with a large packet. "Hi, I'm here to explain this Hazmat Containment Kit, in case your bag springs a leak." He went on to explain that the kit contained surgical gown, gloves, and mask, and then there was a tarp, and specialty towels for absorbing the chemicals. He made it clear that touching the chemicals was to be avoided at all costs. Once again, I looked up at the IV bag

slowly dripping into my chest, and felt a ripple of fear. That clear liquid in there would burn through my hand, yet it's being pumped into
my body? Not a good feeling. And holy crap, what if it burst open in
my car? I imagined it could eat right through the seats and floor before
I had a chance to pull over.

I hadn't recovered from Hazmat Boy when another lab tech
appeared with my new drug pump satchel. She showed me how to
slip the IV bag into the inner pocket, and wrap it in Velcro straps. I
wasn't to touch the IV cord more than necessary, since the other end
of it was now snugly taped to my chest port. "Oh," she remembered,
"by the way, no showering this week, okay? You don't want to get your
port site wet. We'll bandage it up, but it has to stay dry." *Whack.*

Here's the thing about what I called the "Satchel of Death"—I
am not a good purse carrier. I've always had bad luck remembering them, and on the days I've tried, I am forever backtracking to
retrieve them from chairs, or restaurants, friends' cars or bathroom
stalls. Like umbrellas, for me, purses are too often single-use items.
So walking out of the hospital with the messenger bag casually slung
over my shoulder, I had every horrific vision possible. What if I got
out of the car and it was on the passenger seat, and I slammed the car
door? What if I had it on the back of a chair, and then walked away?
And how on earth would I sleep without yanking the needle out of
my chest?

While these bad scenes played out in my brain, I was heading
north in the car. Of all weeks, *this* week I'd agreed to house- and cat-sit
for a friend from the choir, whose home was up on one of the Vermont
islands. (Yes, Vermont has islands. They are lovely. You should check
them out.) Ironically, when I'd only had to go to the hospital once in
the week, I was living ten minutes away, but this week, when I had to
go every day, I'd be a full hour away. Nevertheless, I took comfort in
the fact that driving has always been one of my favorite ways to relax;
the scenery is breathtakingly lovely as you leave behind the mountains around Burlington, head up the highway, cross the causeway

into Lake Champlain, and then continue through the rural towns of South Hero and Grand Isle.

I arrived at my friend's house, slipped the key into the lock, greeted the kitty, and went into the living room. Windows on three sides opened right onto the lake, which was huge and blue and crashing like surf on the rocks right below. I stood looking out, but instead of feeling my usual delight at the view, suddenly all the internal walls I'd leaned on in order to get through that awful day just disintegrated. I sat down and cried till I thought I'd die of dehydration. The kitty came to sit with me, a little worried about whether I'd pull myself together in time for her dinner. Still shaky on my legs, I picked up the Satchel of Death, and went to the kitchen to get her food.

After she was settled, I went back to the living room. The pump in the satchel made a tiny *click-whir* sound each time it pumped. I was starting to freak out listening to it, utterly horrified, imagining that each *click-whir* meant "*poison . . . poison . . . poison.*" Finally I gave up and went into the guest room. Slowly and strangely, I started undressing, figuring out how to remove clothes without hitting the IV cord. The satchel lay on the bed, clicking and whirring, and I stood there in dismay, feeling the creepy wrongness of having something outside my body connected straight to my heart. It wasn't right. It just wasn't *right*.

I fell into a deep sleep, exhausted, waking only once. I listened for a while to the pump, and cried some more. In the morning, I took my coffee (and the omnipresent Satchel of Death) out onto the deck, breathed in its aroma mixed with the fresh lake air, and closed my eyes. A reverie came to me, listening to the sloshing of the water, and the sloshing of the drugs. If I listened, I could imagine that the sloshing was all part of a whole, that I was one with the lake and the sky, and that the drugs were sloshing inside me as the lake sloshed around me. The sound of the lake soothed some deep piece of my hurt from the day before, and I was able to relax my shoulders for the first time, taking a deep breath. I turned to my playlist and booted up Peter

Gabriel's "Here Comes the Flood." If you can't fight the rising water, you may as well jump in and swim. It was going to be all right. I was going to be all right.

Then there was the prednisone. A typical dose of prednisone, for an allergy or other adult use, ranges from 5 to 80 mgs per day. People who are on it are carefully tapered off of the drug when they're done, to prevent a prednisone crash. Along with the good things it does, it carries a walloping list of possible side effects, from "aggressive behavior" to "vomiting of material that looks like coffee grounds." Ewww. That's for a typical dosage. The prednisone dose that came with my chemo was 120 mgs, twice a day. 240 mgs a day. And after a week, it simply stopped. No taper.

When my nurse explained to me how revved up it would make me feel, I didn't quite believe her. But when I found myself vacuuming the rug at 3:00 am or looking up from a book, noticing it was dawn outside and that I'd read straight through the night without ever feeling sleepy, I realized that stuff had some pretty serious clout. I'd been given sleeping pills also; I was to take the prednisone earlier in the evening and the sleeping pill when I was ready to call it a day. Jefferson Airplane's classic song "White Rabbit" from the psychedelic 1960s would run through my head as I reached for one or the other of my bottles. I ended up labeling the pills "Up" and "Down," depending which direction I wanted to be heading next. I was reminded of a snippet of Psalm 139:

> It's a fact: darkness isn't dark to you; night and day, darkness
> and light, they're all the same to you. (*The Message*)

More and more often, I found I had to look outside to remind myself whether it was day or night. The chemistry experiment that was my body needed more cues in order to orient itself with the moment.

The day before I was unhooked from the satchel, my nurse Kristen wandered into the infusion suite to check on me. "Hey," she began, in a slightly hesitant voice. "Um, there's one other change with this new protocol. The good news is you don't have to come into the clinic the day after chemo to get your booster shot for your white blood cells." Huh. I could tell another shoe was about to drop. "Um, instead, you'll get a couple of packs of prefilled syringes, and you can just self-inject them for ten days yourself, at home." She said this in a voice that was trying hard to make it sound like I'd won some sort of chemo lottery. Yay, you get to self-inject for ten days—that's *so* much better than coming to the cheery clinic for that one shot.

I stared at her. I was the kid who had had to be dragged screaming out from under the table at the pediatrician's when I got a shot. I was the kid who, every single time I was on my way to the doctor, had fantasized about leaping out of the car at each stop sign or stop light, terrified even by the *thought* of getting a shot. (I once did pop the car door open at a red light, but my mother's furious response assured that I never tried the escape-hatch-route again.) Yes, I was supposedly a grown-up now, and yes, I had endured countless injections, infusions, IVs, and blood draws in the past few months. But that was a very, very far cry from me sticking something through my own beloved flesh. Dear God, let there be another way.

"Don't worry," Kristen said. "I'll go get a sample now and we can practice. Really, there's nothing to it."

What do you imagine when you visualize practicing giving an injection? Maybe Kristen would come back with saline, and we'd give each other shots? Maybe I'd practice doing it to myself? Huh.

Actually, the practice involved injecting water into something that looked very much like one of those breast self-exam flesh-blobs. This one was not shaped like a breast; it was just a faux-skin injection pad. I was fine stabbing it and pushing the plunger, but I was not assured that this was going to be doable when the syringe was aimed at *me*.

Kristen, as always, was a brick. "Here," she said, "place your hand over your belly button. Don't aim for within that area, aim around it. The nerve endings aren't so close as you get further away, and you won't feel it as much. Oh, and after you swipe the site with the alcohol wipe, give your skin a chance to dry off for a minute. Lots of the sting you feel is just from the alcohol in the injection site, if it's still wet." I was armed with mountains of her good advice, and her assurance that I was up for this.

Next in line came someone from the lab, carrying the boxes of pre-filled syringes. "These aren't shelf-stable, so keep them in the refrigerator. But you don't want to inject them cold; take one out about half an hour beforehand and let it warm up a bit." The nurses came over to check them out. "Did you get the beveled kind?" "I hope you got bevel-ended ones?" Again I was a lottery winner—I had beveled syringes. One minute you're incredulous that they expect you to inject yourself, and the next minute everyone is clapping you on the back, and telling you that those are the "good" needles, and you won't feel a thing. I admit, my ability to celebrate the bevels was mitigated by my complete lack of confidence that I was ever, *ever* going to actually use one of these. Even in high school biology, when we'd had to prick our own fingers so we could look at our blood under the microscopes, I'd bribed my lab partner to give me a drop of her blood after staring at my finger and the mini-lancet for more than ten minutes without moving.

After five days, they unplugged the IV tubing. The insanely high prednisone dose had given me what they call "moon face." I woke up on Saturday morning looking inflated. I felt lousy. I looked worse. I almost crawled back under the covers to spend the entire weekend in hiding.

But I didn't. I forced myself to check the local paper to see if there was anything going on around town that would keep me out of the house and distracted. Oh, look, it's the Champlain Valley Fair; this was just what I needed, to find a place where I could go be anony-mous, in a crowd. As a gregarious introvert, sometimes a festive gath-ering of strangers can be counted on to cheer me up when I'm feeling lost or lonely.

Only after I'd paid for my parking, only after I'd walked from the lot to the fair in the hot August sun, only after I'd purchased my entry ticket, did it occur to me that two things I was supposed to avoid were (1) large crowds and (2) livestock. Oh, great. Totally forgot that. Deep down, I was still so angry about the tumor not dying, I felt defiant, as if misbehaving or getting really sick would somehow be an adult way to register my displeasure.

Nevertheless, walking around in the crowds worked its usual magic. Listening to families banter, watching kids race by, the noise and the rides and the exhibits did me a lot of good. In no time, I had been drawn out of myself and was feeling better than I had all week. As I felt sunburn starting on my arms, I remembered a third thing I was meant to do: stay out of direct sunlight. Well, hell. It was too late for that, too. It just felt so good to blend into the crowd and pass, for this day, as a typical person at the fair, not afraid of dying, not worried about side effects or meds. I felt giddy with freedom now that the Satchel of Death had been turned back in, and nothing was being pumped into my heart except my own blood.

And of course, I ended up with the livestock. A fair isn't complete until you've seen the sheep and piglets. One of the performers in a small ring that day was a tiny piglet named Sophie, whose great talent was swimming across a baby pool to get an Oreo. Could there be anything cuter? I laughed watching her, as I hadn't laughed in ages, and even held her and had our picture taken together. Oh—weren't swine one of the *specific* things I was not supposed to touch? Whatever. Looking into Sophie's bright eyes, I figured it was worth every risk. I resisted kissing her tiny pink snout, but only just barely.

Finally, I walked into the fiber arts building, where knitted items were on display. There was a small circle of folks sitting at spinning wheels in the middle of the room, happily spinning away. A kindly older gentleman looked up at me and said, "Are you Maureen? Would you be able to come back tomorrow and be a part of the spinning demo? I don't have enough people signed up." I smiled back and said,

"Well, sir, I'm not Maureen, but I do spin, and I'd love to join you tomorrow if the offer still stands?"

We laughed and introduced ourselves, and he welcomed me to come sit with the others in the morning, and spend the day spinning in public and answering questions or teaching visitors how the wheels worked.

So, nursing my sunburn, crashing off my prednisone, and with a perfectly round face that highlighted the recent loss of my eyebrows, I was back in the morning with my spinning wheel. By the end of that second long fair day, I was fully exhausted, but I had spent eight hours chatting with people, with no time for myself or my own worries. That was perhaps the best therapy I could have asked for, and as I stumbled back to the car with my wheel, I gave thanks again for the serendipity that had brought me out to the fair, and given me two days of such pleasure.

So, back to the shots.

As ever, I prepared by gathering a playlist on my phone for the injections. Then that first morning, I devised the following plan of attack: I would make my morning coffee, and then I would sit at the coffee table with my coffee ready but untouched before me. Nothing makes me as sad as lukewarm coffee, so I figured this setup would force me to inject quickly.

Plan:

1. Take shot out of fridge to warm up
2. Make coffee
3. Pick playlist song for the day
4. Lay out materials on coffee table with fresh cup of coffee
5. Swab tummy with alcohol and fan to dry
6. Turn on song to get psyched
7. Do the thing
8. Rejoice and drink coffee

Pretty foolproof, right? The first morning, I felt like I was juggling fifteen balls in the air. I hit my phone, and a steel drum introduced Bob Marley, singing "I Shot the Sheriff." The area was prepped and ready, and I ripped the packaging off the syringe. Oh, right, I have to pull this cap off the needle part. . . done. . . oh God, there's the needle. Don't look. Don't look. Holding it like Kristen had showed me, like a pen, I breathed slowly and deeply. Do it. . . do it. . . C'mon, Crick— your coffee's getting cold—*do it*.

Adulting. Nobody had ever said it would be like this. That you would find yourself sitting at your coffee table on a summer morning holding a syringe and staring at your stomach. But I knew that the longer I postponed this, the more freaked I would get, and the more my coffee would cool off. Okay, let's do this thing.

And you know what? That beveled end? I hardly noticed it. Seriously, I swung it at my tummy and it was in. OK, push the plunger gently but firmly, there, that's it, that's all. Pull out. . . pull out—ah, you did it. As the steel drums continued in the background, Bob was swearing that the shot was in self-defense. Amen to that, Bob. Amen to that. A little shaken, but relieved, I carefully tucked the syringe into an empty bleach bottle that would be my "sharps" container, and then reached for my coffee. Nice. Still hot.

Sometime in the second week, I was preparing my syringe zone, booting up "Hit Me With Your Best Shot," and waiting for the coffee to brew. I puttered around my tiny apartment a little, but something seemed to be wrong with the coffee maker. There clearly wasn't any coffee brewing. I went over to the machine and pulled out the pot, and there it was. Coffee. But, I hadn't smelled anything. I drink jet black Sumatran dark roast, and the scent of it in the morning is one of my deepest pleasures. I tipped my head over the pot and breathed in again. Nothing. Not a thing.

Holy crap. Turning around, I pulled open the fridge and took out a jar of pesto. I screwed off the lid and brought the jar to my nose. Nothing. Frantic, I ran into the bathroom to find the most invasive scent I could, a jar of Vicks VapoRub. It had no smell whatsoever. Or, more accurately, *I couldn't smell a thing.* They had warned me about this possible side effect, but until it happens you have no idea how devastating it is. Staring stupidly into the Vicks, I started to cry. I kept sniffing and sniffing, as if perhaps, like a light switch, my sense of smell would just snap back, but of course it doesn't work that way.

Back in the kitchen, I raised the coffee cup to my mouth (violating, just this once, the order of my liturgy of injection), but I tasted nothing. It was all gone. Nearby on the counter was a bowl of peanut M&M's. Nervously, I took a few, placed them in my mouth, and chewed. Nope. It was like having a mouth full of sawdust. I had to spit them out. *I just spat out M&M's.* Holding my now-cooled coffee, I went back to the couch and sat down. I had not seen this coming. *Whack.*

It turned out to be a fluke that both of these senses went at the same time. Later in the month, actually just a few days before the next infusion, my taste buds slowly perked up, but my sense of smell stayed dead until well after the chemo ended. However, without smell, your ability to notice and differentiate among tastes is compromised. Yes, your taste buds can distinguish broad flavors like salty and sweet, but it is your sense of smell that adds all the nuance. Working together, scents and tastes are rich and multilayered. Taste without smell is a flat experience. It would be months before my coffee tasted like anything more than hot water. Eating became the most boring exercise, an endless chewing and swallowing of sawdust.

Then there was the peripheral neuropathy, which means numbness in your extremities; for me, toes and fingers. Suddenly, I just got clumsy. I was forever dropping pens, or my knitting, or once even my morning injection (which of course landed squarely in the top of my foot). I just never knew if I had hold of things. My toes felt as though my socks had bunched up in the ends of my shoes. For weeks I kept taking off my shoes to see what was wrong. Was there something stuffed into the toes of my sneakers? Were my socks weirdly bunched? No. I finally realized that because I couldn't feel my toes, the rest of my foot felt them as an "obstruction" at the ends of my shoes, as if they were an intruder, and not actually a part of my body. Like in Oliver Sacks's terrific book, *The Man Who Mistook His Wife for a Hat*, I suddenly had a tiny taste of what it felt like when your brain no longer recognized a part of your own body. There were completely different reasons behind the issues, of course—I did not have a neurological issue in my brain; I simply had nerve endings in my toes that no longer received or sent messages.

At the time of writing this book, three and a half years after my treatment ended, I still have two totally numb toes. Everything else has come back. At first, I was annoyed at them, but now I use them as a tiny gratitude reminder. Every day when I put on my shoes, they remind me that two numb toes are a small price to pay for being alive.

～～～

Please call me by my true names,
so I can hear all my cries and laughter at once,
so I can see that my joy and pain are one.
Please call me by my true names,
so I can wake up
and the door of my heart
could be left open,
the door of compassion.[17]

—Thich Nhat Hanh

Wednesday of that week, I was scheduled to celebrate the Healing Service at the cathedral. The folks who came to this service were beautifully broken and open-hearted, and I had seen through the year how they supported one another, and offered themselves to one another as

17. Thich Nhat Hanh, "Call Me By My True Names," in *Call Me By My True Names: The Collected Poems* (Berkeley: Parallax Press, 1999), 72–73.

well as to visitors and total strangers. They were risk-takers for love, and being with them was deeply healing and inspirational.

And yet, I found myself in a tailspin trying to figure out what to do with the Satchel. It seemed to me a little tacky (the great Episcopal sin) to simply sling the messenger bag on over my alb, stole, body mic, and chasuble, as if I'd vested for worship and then was planning on a little shopping afterward. I had choices about wearing it underneath one layer, or all of my layers, but even swathed in large expanses of white cotton and gloriously embroidered silk, the pack pooched out in a freaky, Quasimodo-like way. While my good folks waited in their seats for the service to start, I was hiding in the vesting room, nervously adjusting the wig, and trying to hang the bag on my body so I didn't yank the IV cord from my chest and didn't have a bizarre bulge appearing from under my robes.

It's funny how we judge ourselves. Nobody was going to care whether my robes hung symmetrically or not. Why was I whipping myself up into such a tizzy? In my heart I know it is always so hard to expose myself, my own softness. It was one thing for me to pray for healing in the midst of these folks, to lay my hands on them and pray from my heart for light, and grace, and love. It had taken me to a place of frightening intimacy and vulnerability to admit that I had cancer and needed their prayers, and then take my own turn sitting in the central chair at these services, while they laid their hands on me and prayed with wisdom and tenderness. Now my illness was on full display, and the only person who was incapable of looking at my woundedness was me.

In a note to Max, my therapist, the next day, this is how I described it:

I was celebrating the Healing Service at the cathedral on Wednesday, and feeling mighty self-conscious about having that whirring chemo pack strapped on over my flowing robes and stole and chasuble . . . so before I started the service, I came out and said, "As most of you know, I'm in the middle

of chemotherapy, and this week they've changed my routine a
bit, so I have to wear this pack all week. I hope it won't be too
distracting—"

As if rehearsed, a guy in the front row pulled up his t-shirt
and said, "Hey, I have an implanted insulin pump!" Across the
aisle, another guy pulled up the leg of his shorts and said, "I've
got a bladder bag strapped to my leg!" A woman behind him
yanked down her top to show us her heart valve scar. It happened so fast, and they were all beaming like first-graders at
show-and-tell.

There was a beat of silence, and we all dissolved into roars
of laughter. It does seem that the things we are most afraid of,
which seem like they separate us from others, are precisely the
things that bring us closer together. We just laughed and laughed
at all of our appendages and wounds. By the end we had tears
rolling down our cheeks at being such fragile, funny animals.

Please, call me by my true names.

What is hardest is sitting with our fear, *before* we break. After
the breaking, we have space for blessing and goodness to fill us, and
heal us.

Zen Mountain Monastery

I was pretty nervous about the "Introduction to Zen" weekend at Zen Mountain Monastery. Although this was what I had been most looking forward to—a visit to a community entirely different from those in which I'd grown up—I think the awkwardness of my KTD visit had left me wary of trying to step unnoticed into another religious tradition like a chameleon. For an entire week beforehand, I wondered if perhaps I should skip it. Their website laid out the schedule clearly: wake-up gong at 4:50 am, meditation and worship for ninety minutes before breakfast, work duty, hours of seated meditation, sleeping in bunk beds in dorm rooms. . . I found myself struggling between my desire for predictability and comfort and my desire for this spiritual challenge. Even though intellectually I was curious and interested in learning more about Zen Buddhism, as the weekend grew closer an anxious inner voice tried to talk me out of going.

Throughout my chemo months, this became a familiar struggle. I was learning, over and over again, that *what I told myself* about how I "might" feel or what "might" be easy or challenging could quickly become my reality. When the pessimistic strain of self-talk got the better of me, I could feel myself withdrawing from other people and from experiences that would engage and energize me. Now, with the added stress of wearing the chemo pack all week, followed by the ten days of self-injections, and the reality that I was feeling more physically fragile as a result of the new combination of drugs, I was even more hesitant. Under the pretense of "saving my energy," or "protecting myself from germs," I could easily talk myself out of doing anything—even if it was something I wanted to do. So it was with this fourth pilgrimage. As exciting as it had been to plan these trips, as they grew closer, my brain fought me. It played the cancer card, telling me that I was sick and should stay home. Over and over, I had to fight back my reluctance, my worry, my fear, and trust that the original impulse to get out of my apartment and engage with strangers and friends was the *real* choice I wanted to make. Over and over, I had to ignore that voice that tried to tell me I wasn't up to these pilgrimages. My ongoing work in therapy and with meditation directly challenged this fear-filled conversation. What if I didn't try to imagine how I might feel tomorrow, and just felt what I did in the moment? What if I didn't second-guess how the weekend would go down, and just entered into it as best I could, curious about the experience as it unfolded?

Zen Mountain Monastery describes itself as "distinctly American," a Western Zen center for teaching as well as an established residential monastery.[18] Founded in 1980 as the Zen Arts Center, ZMM soon grew into a true home for training in the traditions of ancient Chinese and Japanese Zen liturgy and practice. Our modern culture too often dismisses the word "Zen" as being inextricable from the punch line of jokes about "one hand clapping." Having latched onto a few phrases that seem comical or absurd, the deep holy resonances of Zen teachings remain a mystery to many of us.

In my understanding, Zen is to Buddhism what Trappists are to Christian monasticism—a reform movement calling for stricter

---

18. "The Mountains and Rivers Order," https://zmm.mro.org/about/history-of -zmm-and-mro/

observance to the original practices of a faith tradition. Religious groups and movements are susceptible to relating to their founding precepts in ways that can be either too lenient *or* too strict. Think of televangelists, misdirecting funds into luxury cars and mansions, or St. Francis, whose vision for a new monastic lifestyle of abject poverty led to the death by starvation of some of his earliest followers. Reform movements often call for a return to an ideal of silence and contemplation, and less concern about worldly comforts, even at times erring on the side of discomfort (hair shirt, anyone?). In my nervous mind I argued that chemo was enough of a mortification. Did I really need to go looking for ways to beat myself up physically, in order to connect more deeply spiritually?

Such was my internal dialogue before I left Vermont. I had a five-hour trip, during which I could alternately enjoy the drive and worry about the weekend. It was a hot Friday in September, and I was nervous about the people I'd be with. A Zen monastery in Woodstock, New York, brought to mind either elderly hippies long since mind-blown on too much acid, or intense, urban New Yorkers looking for a quick spiritual connection. Who on earth goes to "Introduction to Zen" weekend, really?

Finally pulling into the driveway, I marveled at the large property. In the back, a significant construction project was underway. I headed to the far end of the parking lot, and sat in my car for a few moments, breathing deeply and trying to let go of my anxiety.

This happens to me with surprising frequency. I'll have a huge plan to which I become deeply attached, I'll make details align so I can live into that plan, and then at the very brink of the plan's actualization, I'll freeze and wonder: "What was I thinking?" This is why, after planning ahead for three months and after five hours of driving, in the shade of the monastery, I sat in the car having second thoughts. One of my concerns was my wig. On the three earlier pilgrimages, I'd had my own private room. How would I sleep in a room with other people and Harriet, the wig? Would I try to sleep while wearing it? If

I took it off, would that creep people out? Nobody had seen me bald, not even my doctors and nurses. Plus, it was hot and humid, and it was slipping around a bit. Things were bound to get weird.

I did not have one of those admirably glossy scalps like the people who have shaved their heads. Mine sprouted some thin strands of hair that had stubbornly refused to give up. It was like the random stubble of a Maine blueberry field after sections had been burned off, patchy and rough. I had been warned by several hair stylists not to shave it, to prevent painful ingrown hairs and to prevent irritating the tender scalp skin that throbbed and ached.

Oh well. I could delay no longer. Better to get inside and at least see where I'd be sleeping and get a feel for the place before the program swung into full gear. Grabbing my duffle bag, I locked the car and walked toward the building.

And there, on the large back wall, looking bizarrely both at home and out of place, hung a massive, carved wooden crucifix. Jesus, somewhat apologetically, hung on the cross as if to say, "Uh, yeah, I know this is a Buddhist monastery—awkward." Huh. My first thought was that I had accidentally turned into the wrong driveway. But no, there by the doors was a Buddha statue, and a string of flapping prayer flags. This was the place. *Odd.*

I came into the entry and turned down the stairs as directed to the registration area. As I clattered down the final few steps, several nuns ranging in age from their mid-twenties to mid-eighties looked up expectantly. They were readying materials and setting out room assignments on long tables, and at the sound of my feet each one looked up with a smile.

I stopped, transfixed: every woman in the room was bald.

Well, yes. I suppose I should have seen that coming, but I'd been so hooked by my own nerves that I hadn't considered it. This is a Buddhist monastery—the monks and nuns will have shaved their heads.

I must have looked funny, frozen at the bottom step, with my head cocked and my mouth open. The nuns looked back, curious and smiling. "Oh," I said, "I was just sitting in the car wondering if I ought to wear this, but now I realize I don't have to." I raised my hand to my head, and slid off the wig, looking shyly back at the nuns. Their smiles broadened, as I stood there with my bald, rough scalp exposed. "Welcome," one of the young sisters said as she stepped forward and wrapped me into a hug. "Welcome to Zen Mountain Monastery."

Once again, all of my worry melted away, and I felt myself relax into this surprising place where a stranger was welcomed like a beloved family member. Suddenly, their having Jesus hanging on the back wall of the building also made sense. *Everyone* was welcome here. Their reach was broad enough to enfold us all, friend and stranger, patient and prophet.

I was assigned to a tiny room upstairs, which miraculously contained five bunk beds and a bathroom. I snagged a top bunk in a corner, and clambered up to make the bed and lay out a few personal items: my pillow, pjs, and journal. Climbing back down, I stared for a minute at the wig. Yes? No? I hadn't "gone bald" before, not anywhere. A glance in the bathroom mirror confirmed the worst: my baldness did not project the glossy serenity of the nuns. My scalp was patchy and dull. My head looked dejected. "Oh, what the hell," I figured, and tucked the wig gently into my duffle bag, feeling like I was ditching a pal at a sleepover. "You get the weekend off, my friend." If I was going to be fully here, I was ready to let something go.

Since I was registered and unpacked, I had some free time to explore the grounds. It was a beautiful day, and the setting of the monastery between two rivers, at the base of Tremper Mountain, made walking outside seem like meditation. The feeling of the sun on my uncovered scalp was startling, and I reached up frequently to run a gentle hand over my head and soothe it. "It's okay, little one, you're okay here." I looped through the meadows and paths, examined the construction site of a new, eco-friendly building, watched other cars roll into the parking area as my fellow retreatants arrived, and sat by the garden, listening to the wind and the birds. As if in slow motion,

I felt myself arrive again. I was feeling more calm and curious, more able to open my heart to this weekend. Nature had done her work on my jangled nerves, and I was ready.

Walking back toward the main building, I saw that my path was on a trajectory that would link up to the path of another walker, as one of the monks was coming in from the garden. Unsure of how to greet him, or whether perhaps he simply wanted to keep silence, I slowed my steps and looked inquiringly at him. He too looked up, caught my eye, and smiled, indicating with a gentle movement of his hand that we might walk together.

Although raised in a gregarious family, I find myself often shy with strangers. I dipped my head in acknowledgment, and allowed my path to align with that of the monk's. He smiled kindly back, but without the usual need either to introduce himself or ask me who I was. We walked a little way in silence, before he pointed up to the crucifix on the back wall. "Have you heard the story about that sculpture?" he asked.

"No, I haven't," I said. "But I would love to. I can't decide if he seems out of place or at home there."

The monk laughed. "Yes. Both." He told me that the building had originally been built by a Catholic priest, and had been used for retreats and other religious gatherings. The crucifix had been a part of the original building. Sadly, the retreat house fell into disuse, and then sat empty and neglected for a time, before it was put on the market.

"When we first purchased the property, that back wall was plain. We went about fixing up the building and walking the land to get to know it. One day, deep in the woods, some members of the community came across that sculpture, standing in the woods. Some locals had dragged it out there, and were using it for target practice. He was in a sorry state. Returning to the monastery to describe what they had found, others recalled the shadow on the back outdoor wall, where the building had retained an outline of the sculpture because it had shielded the wall from years of weather and sun. Unanimously, they voted to restore the sculpture, and replace it on the wall as a sign of respect."

I was gobsmacked. Buddhists hanging a sculpture of Jesus on their building to honor him? Suddenly I understood more deeply that the false walls we build in ourselves and in our communities—the ones that pretend that there are separate teams, that there is an "us" and a "them"—that all of these walls and boundary lines are *imaginary*. There is no "us" and "them." There is only *us*. This smiling, thoughtful man unfolded the story as though it had been the most natural thing in the world to replace Jesus on the back wall. My head rang with all of the squabbles I had witnessed during decades in parish priesthood, the turf wars, the wrangling, the arguments about scarce resources, the competition or power struggles between clergy or parishes. How sad, how silly. Our divisions only exist in our minds.

Suddenly, an echo of the word *Namaste* sounded deep in my heart: "I bow to the Divine in you." Walking with this monk, I caught a glimpse of a world in which people are not threatened by the Light in each other, are neither defensive nor frightened when encountering something that is different from their own experience or tradition. Here at Zen Mountain Monastery, *Namaste* was not just a word. It was how they lived.

Our first task of the weekend was supper, a light meal consisting mainly of salads and grains. The round tables filled quickly with visitors and monks and nuns, all chatting merrily. Hands extended across plates of food, as people introduced themselves. My foolish expectations about who would be joining me on the weekend were immediately doused. To my left was seated a woman from Paris who had come for a month-long retreat, and to my right was seated the monk with whom I'd walked back from the gardens. As conversation picked up, I realized that the monk was the abbot of the community, Ryushin Sensei. Peppered with questions about himself, how he had come to the monastery, what his life had been beforehand, this large-hearted man laughed frequently while speaking with simplicity about his unusual path, from a childhood in Poland, to an anthropology degree at Yale, to service in the US Navy, then medical school and practice as a pediatrician and a psychiatrist, to following the dharma. Sensei (the preferred form of address for a teacher, like "Professor" or "Rabbi") was in turns deeply self-reflective, playful, curious about the others at the table, and inspiring. Around the table, people from different countries were easily drawn together into community by this magnetic man. The meal reminded me of those I'd shared years before, staying in youth hostels while backpacking around Europe. I'd sit down to eat with a collection of total strangers and, hours later, we would stand up after the meal laughing and looking deeply into one another's eyes, as friends who might not even share a common language but who had forged a common bond.

The evening's introduction to the weekend went quickly after this, and soon we found ourselves hurrying into bed, to prepare for that early morning gong. Five bunk beds, ten women, one bathroom. There was a silent dance of courtesy, as we all moved in and around each other, and finally into our beds. After the emotional work of the day, I was sound asleep before my head sank fully into my pillow.

Thwok. Thwok. Tok. . . tok. . . tok, tok, tok, toktoktoktoktok!
My first thought, in the deep darkness, was that someone had dropped something in the hallway in the middle of the night. It sounded like a piece of wood had been dropped on the hard wood floor, over and over. But then, as the hollow wooden sound continued, speeding up, I realized this was our wake-up gong, actually called a *han*. The rhythmic knocking of a wooden mallet on a wooden board was easier on the ears than a loud bell or alarm clock might have been, even though I am hard-pressed to say I was *glad* to be awakened at 4:50 am. Nevertheless, I knew this was where my emotional rubber would hit the road. How I chose to respond in this predawn moment would color my entire day. I quickly clambered down from my bunk,

brushed my teeth in silence, and made my stupefied way with many others through the darkened hallways and staircases toward morning meditation.

And, oh—there was coffee.

It is very hard for me to say how touching I found this, since I was expecting to have to deny myself the simple comforts (or crutches) that make life somewhat easier. But Zen Mountain Monastery is, in every way, a place of lovingkindness, and so moving through the dimly lit dining room on the way to the zendo for meditation, we were given just enough time to grab a fresh cup of stunningly strong coffee and enjoy it before moving on. I held the mug to my heart, and breathed in and out my gratitude, sending prayers for ease and health to myself, my fellow retreatants, my oncology team, my family, and all who were suffering in the world. "May the joy and love I feel in this cup be also with you, this day, in whatever you encounter." The practice of sending out gratitude for my own life to others who might need encouragement or peace is such a simple prayer, and one I continue to use every morning in that sweet pause before I take my first sip of coffee.

The zendo had a stark beauty at that hour. Rows of cushions in perfect symmetry, the lighting dimmed, the deep silence as we stood beside our *zabutons* waiting for the bell to welcome us to our cushions and the morning *zazen* practice.

Our teachers had explained to us that the practice would be broken into sections of lengthy seated meditation time, with shorter breaks for walking meditation. The hope was that you would move seamlessly from one of these to the next, but we had been told that bathroom breaks, if absolutely necessary, could be taken quickly during the walking portions of the morning. Just knowing it was permissible to take care of these bodily needs meant we didn't have to feel anxiety over them.

We had also been instructed in dealing with discomfort during seated meditation. In other, less formal groups I'd been with, it was

allowable to shift a position if you were suffering from significant discomfort. You could quietly uncross and recross your legs, for example, if that might alleviate the pressure or issue. At Zen Mountain
Monastery, we were instead invited to acknowledge the discomfort
and then try to let it go, without moving. "Yes, knee, you are feeling
sore there. I acknowledge you, but I'm not going to move." We were
not told that we could not, under any circumstances, shift an inch,
but we were *invited* not to move as a discipline. If ignoring the leg or
foot or shoulder seemed impossible, then instead try to focus all of the
mind on the area. Be curious, and ask questions. What exactly did it
feel like—what were the sensations? Pain is not just one thing, always
the same. Did it feel prickly? Was it a slow burning sensation? Were
there stabbing pains, and what happened then in between the stabs?
Was there relief? Was there throbbing? In a bizarre twist, trying to get
inside of the pain, for me, frequently dissolved it on the spot. Trying
to name and dissect the details of the pain, bearing with it, also gave
the pain space to be a piece of my experience without taking over the
entire experience.

After the first night of *zazen*, the rules for stillness tightened up.
While sitting on our cushions in the morning, suddenly a monk in the
back who was keeping an eye on the entire gathering would yell out
sharply, "No moving in the zendo!" I was shocked, like a first grader
when someone openly disobeyed a rule. Someone moved? Who was
it? How much did he or she move? Did *I* move? It was a tad alarming.
With each meditation session the monks pushed us to a deeper level,
so we could experience and absorb it in stages.

Does this line of thinking make you cringe? How can it not,
when we have been taught to stand up for ourselves, take care of
ourselves, avoid pain and not put up with anything that impinges
on our own happiness? I like how Pema Chödrön says it: "There's a
common misunderstanding among all the human beings who have
ever been born on the earth that the best way to live is to try to avoid

pain and just try to get comfortable." [19] "Getting comfortable" is our way of running away from the present moment. If I can learn to sit on my cushion when my nose itches, or my knee aches, or my foot falls slowly and painfully to sleep, and *not have to fix it immediately*, then I can learn to be equally fearless and constant in other arenas in my life. Everything that happens on the cushion is a rehearsal for everything that happens off of it. When I asked the abbot over dinner how he would define "Zen," his answer was, "Zen is the wisdom of no escape."

Another definition I learned over the weekend was the definition of suffering. Suffering is the distance between how things are in the present moment, and how we *wish they were*. If in the present moment I am ill and I can accept being ill, then there isn't much room for suffering. I may experience pain, but I don't have to suffer. But if instead I am sick and I am also angry that my body isn't healing fast enough, and I am sad that I won't be able to go to a certain party or gathering, and I am scared that I might not get better—all of these emotions focus on things that are not present in the moment; the more distance I create between where I simply am and what I want instead, the more I suffer. Zen is having this wisdom: that we can't escape what is real in this one moment, and so we must not try. Too often our impulses will encourage us to flee from pain, whether physical or mental or emotional, by medicating ourselves with opiates or alcohol or sex or food or extreme physical activity or gambling or you name it. Others try to flee literally, and simply walk away from the moment. Instead of self-medicating, they might leave the room, the relationship, the country. In either case, the avoidance of the moment creates distance, because we can soothe ourselves with something that distracts us, avoiding the discomfort.

---

19. Pema Chödrön, *The Wisdom of No Escape: How to Love Yourself and Your World* (London: Element, 2004), 1.

The problem is, though, that life will continue to throw us curveball. We will be unhappy again. So if we reached for a crutch the last time, we set ourselves up to look for that same crutch the next time we find ourselves struggling. Just one more drink, one more bet, one more pill. If instead there is no escape, we can learn to find the strength to stay with it. If I can sit on my cushion for an entire forty-five minutes and not shift my position in the face of significant discomfort, then perhaps the next time something challenges me in another aspect of my life, I will have the courage not to run, not to escape, and not to have to fix it. Zen training, and seated meditation in general, is training for the courage to show up, fully awake, in your own life. The more you do that, the more beautiful your experience of your life can be, and the less your happiness depends on external events.

Though we were invited not to move, the monks offered us a concession by way of a warning. We were reminded to move in a slow, mindful fashion throughout the weekend, but especially to honor our bodies as we switched between seated and walking meditation. We were told that, should we find that a foot or leg had fallen asleep during meditation, we should remain on our *zabuton* as feeling came back to it, and then join as able in the walking. A recent retreatant, ignoring this advice, had stood up and taken one step before crashing to the ground, having no feeling in his left leg. Care for the whole community was to be our first thought, and staying seated on our cushion was infinitely preferable to creating a major disturbance and possibly injuring ourselves.

This was to serve me well, for in the months I had been practicing meditation I had encountered the recurring issue of my right leg falling asleep. I don't have the flexibility for full- or even half-lotus sitting postures, but a simple cross-legged style can still put enough pressure on nerves to send body parts to sleep. That first morning, when the gong rang for us to stand up and begin walking meditation, I unfolded my legs and realized I had no feeling at all from my right toes practically up to my belly button. It felt like even my hip had nodded off. Therefore, I spent most of the first walking break gently rubbing the leg to get some feeling back, while the others walked in a measured procession around the edges of our meditation space.

Following the morning prayer service, I snuck away to the basement, where I had been given permission to stow my syringes in an employee refrigerator. I smiled at the incongruity of the situation while I sat in a stall in the ladies' room waiting for the medicine to warm up. Whose life was this, I wondered, as I tucked the syringe into the crook of my armpit to warm it up while I set up my injection supplies on my knee. And how could it be that, having given myself that first shot only five days earlier, now I did it like a pro, wiping the alcohol towelette across my stomach, pulling the cap off the needle, popping that beveled end through my skin with a quick snap, and plunging the medicine in? When I had argued and cried and balked about not wanting to do it, I had suffered quite a bit, but when I just *did it*, there was no suffering at all. I was beginning to understand the wisdom of no escape, and was back in the breakfast room with a cup of coffee before I knew it.

Following breakfast, we all had chores to do. I had sent up a prayer that, because of my low white blood cell count, I wouldn't be assigned to toilet cleaning, so of course that was precisely the thing that I was assigned. No escape. I considered asking quietly for a different job, playing the cancer card in order to make myself more comfortable, but in the end I chose to clean toilets with calm intention. I was swathed in gloves and apron, and armed with eco-friendly disinfectants. It was fine.

In our afternoon session with our teachers, one of the participants asked if he might go get his journal from his car, to take notes during the teaching. The young Zen novice who was leading our conversation tipped her head to one side. "Why would you want to do that?" Several of us laughed, and he explained that if he didn't write down his thoughts, he wouldn't remember them. "Precisely," said the young nun. "They are just your thoughts. They don't really exist. Why would you write them down? You will take away from this weekend the things you really need to learn. They will be written in your body, they will be your lived experience of your time here. What is of value will stay with you. Let the rest go."

Before the evening meditation, we had a brief orientation that asked us to be honest with ourselves about any abuse that we might have suffered, or any trauma that we might be holding due to the abuse of another. This was raised because the next meditation session would introduce use of a *kyosaku*, or "stick of compassion." This is a meditation aid, a long, lightweight stick. Students could request they be smacked sharply with the stick during sitting practice, as an aid to clear the mind, to stay awake, or simply to receive the discipline.

I know, this is where you start looking around for the door, right? But the teachers spoke with great compassion about how nobody would be touched by the stick unless he or she requested it. It is not a punishment, it is a meditation aid. Nevertheless, the stick makes a sharp sound as it is struck on each of a student's shoulders, and the sound alone could trigger someone's memories of abuse. Our teachers were sincerely concerned for our well-being, and let us know that they would make arrangements to sit in a separate space with anyone who needed not to hear or be in the room during this one practice.

To request the stick, you would fold your hands into prayer position while sitting, and wait for the monk to come to you. Then you would bow to request the *kyosaku*, tilting your head to one side to offer one shoulder for the blow. There would be two small taps on your shoulder to alert you, and then the one big smack. The student would then tilt his or her head to the other side, and the procedure was repeated. I was both repelled and intrigued, and I found my meditation distracted with arguments for why I ought to request the blows. But then, honestly, I reminded myself that my body was undergoing a lot of stress already. I bruise easily as it is and, with the crazy assortment of chemicals in my body, my platelets and clotting factors were pretty compromised. I probably did not need to invite these blows at this time. Sitting still in the zendo and hearing the monk's footsteps pause by a neighbor turned out to be enough of a terrifying exercise, waiting to hear the fierce swoosh through the air of the *kyosaku*, and the strong smacking sound as it struck my neighbor's shoulders.

I carry a lot of tension across the tops of my shoulders, and I could see that a well-placed blow to the trapezius muscle might act as an aid to relaxing that tightness. Or, if one were sleepy, that would certainly provide a wake-up. I hungered for the full experience even as the sound was frightening to listen to. In the end, I kept my hands relaxed on my knees, and let the *kyosaku* pass me by.

The "Introduction to Zen" weekend drew to a close before I was ready for it to end. The long periods of sitting mediation were interspersed with teachings, fascinating meal partners, walks on the grounds, and a second night's deep sleep. One monk explained to me that if we swallow down everything we feel throughout the day, then when we finally slow down enough to sleep, we find ourselves processing all of it before we can really rest. I felt very clear and clean in my mind at bedtime, having walked so slowly through each day that every moment was deeply felt.

On my first two pilgrimages, I had felt a deep tie to the monastic communities, and had felt something deeper than mere welcome. I had felt an "at home-ness" that gave me peace and strength. At Zen Mountain Monastery, I left with a better sense of being "at home" in my own body, more at peace with it as it was that very day. I was reminded again that clinging to my own thoughts, worries, and plans for the future was causing me pain, even while it seemed so natural to do. The switch from one chemo regimen to another, for example, had caused me excruciating psychic pain, because I fought the new protocol, fought the doctor's decision, fought the Satchel of Death and the self-administered shots. Now that I had survived all of these, I could see that the actual changes—the shorter chemo days and the flexibility of leaving the hospital carrying my medicine—had made my life a bit easier. What had caused me so much pain was my own fighting against what had to be. What had hurt was a sense that my plans had been changed, a reminder that I was not in control of any of this.

After having weathered a bumpy few weeks, Zen Mountain Monastery handed me back the map that I was trying to follow. Breathe. Feel what you are feeling in your body. Try not to worry too much about what was to come. Enjoy the day at hand. As the young nun had said, "Why would you write down your thoughts? They aren't real. What you need will be written within you." I headed for home knowing that much had been written, and I could take my time rereading and digesting it all with gratitude.

Chemo Round Five

I f I swaggered in for round four, I crawled in for number five.

Through the earlier cycles, I had felt a part of the team. I had felt like we were on the same side, pulling together. But the new drug combination was rougher on me, and I felt battered. My lovely Zen space of "no escape" had escaped. Combine that with the fresh anxiety that this might all be in vain, that the tumor wasn't doing what they'd predicted . . . well, I wasn't in a good place.

I even had written a pleadingly desperate letter to Gianni, trying to illustrate that carrying around the Satchel of Death felt spiritually wounding to me, as opposed to just mildly inconvenient. My page-long plea to go back to the old chemo regime ends with these words:

> . . . after [the pump] was disconnected, I was filled with this overwhelming sense that I'd done something "bad" for me. I can't describe it. I just felt damaged, and that I'd made a bad choice. Even now, I feel shivers of horror thinking about it, and it has snuck into my dreams as well—in a bad way. For the first time since all this started, I could tell that my head wasn't backing the treatment, and that for me is a scary thing. You know me by now—I'm not unreasonable and I'm not negative . . . but I felt pretty freaked out by that treatment.

It was crucial to me that my mind was *with* my body in this cure, and my spirit on board as well. If one part of me doubted, I felt like I didn't have the artillery I needed to beat this thing. I wanted to feel strong, but I felt broken instead.

When I checked in, I wasn't surprised this time to get escorted into the consulting room again. I'm not sure what I was expecting. Would the doctor come in and agree with me? Would he come in and be mad at me? Was I now going to be labeled *that* patient, the difficult one?

But no, it was the PA who came in. He sat next to me and said, "Hey, I saw your note to the doc. We are so sorry that the change in chemo protocol was hard for you. I want to explain a little more about the science here." This, for me, was a good approach. Like when my nurse told me why putting the port catheter straight into my heart was a good idea, because (1) that's where there's the most blood at one time so the caustic chemicals dilute and cause less damage, and (2) that's where the blood moves out into the body the fastest. Oh, OK then. Once it made sense, I could get behind it.

The PA explained that to be perfectly honest, it was much *better* for my body to get the chemo in smaller, slower, daily doses for five days. Yes, listening to the pump was scary, and yes, it felt like the length of time I was hooked up meant I was being slowly poisoned all week, but in reality dripping the chemicals over five days was much gentler on my body than giving me the whole dose in a few hours. Psychologically, it was hard, but if I could get my brain around it, this was actually better for my body.

Oh. All right, then. Satchel of Death wins.

My brother Hap was visiting for this round. I'd told him not to come in early to the hospital, since he was staying at a nice B&B, and sometimes there was a very long wait before things got going. I got settled into the infusion room, and chatted with the nurses while waiting for my drugs to appear.

Once I'd made up my mind to it, I felt 100 percent better. This was how it was going to be. I kept telling myself that this was the better way, the healthier way. Having gotten through round four, I knew I could do it. When the pump got too noisy at night, I knew I could put a pillow over it and ignore it. I knew that there was enough length in the IV tubing that I probably wouldn't pull it out inadvertently. I knew that the chances were pretty good the bag would not rupture, and I wouldn't have to don my Hazmat Kit emergency gear. And this time I was staying nearby, and not house sitting on the island, so I'd be in the neighborhood if I needed backup.

After I got the pack, Hap and I cruised around town, and he was distracting enough that the few days passed quickly, without me obsessing about the satchel or General Malaise[20] too much. Honestly, you really can get used to just about anything, if you put your mind to it. I was deeply appreciative that my PA had taken the time to help me get on board with the new protocol. Attending not only to the chemicals and the bloodwork but also to my fragile feelings and my fear, Fletcher Allen Health Center consistently set itself apart as not just a good hospital, but a great one.

Round five slipped by before I knew it. I got unhooked on Friday, rested up on Saturday, and on Sunday celebrated two services at the cathedral. Stepping into my old shoes, pretending to be my pre-cancer self, was healing from the inside out. Conversation at the coffee hour hovered right where it always does in early fall in Vermont: How's your garden? How's about that weather last week? (This works for good or bad weather.) And, since it was now September, the classic, "Do you think peak will be early this year?" Then followed countless predictions about the peak of foliage season, and everyone's favorite

---

20. Experiencing achy, flu-like symptoms after round four, I told Kristen how I was feeling. She said, "Oh, yes, these drugs can cause general malaise. . ." I replied, "I don't care if he is a general—I'm not saluting him!"

ways of determining which day "peak" would be happening in what place. Favorite prediction methods included reviewing the amount of rain we'd had over the summer, making comparisons to the last foliage season, and noting the stripe-width on woolly bear caterpillars.

As I made my way through the back corridor to take off my robes, I almost bumped into three of my buddies from the choir, laughing over something by the vesting room. I noticed that all three had super short haircuts. I had begun to imagine what it would be like when my own hair grew back, and found myself looking longingly at pictures of Barbara Felton as Agent 99, from the TV show of the late 1960s, *Get Smart*. She had really cute short hair, and I was imagining having her combination of spunk, humor, and hair, someday in the not-too-distant future. "Hey," I said to my pals, "I am really looking forward to joining you three in the Awesome Short Hair Club soon." They looked up, delighted, and one said, "Oh great! Are you getting your hair cut this week?"

Oh. Right. I'd completely forgotten that I hadn't told anyone but the clergy and cathedral organist about the cancer, back in early June. They were professional church staff, and understood keeping confidences. Now here I was with three really good friends, none of whom knew I had been doing chemo and wearing a wig all summer.

Since the choir doesn't sing in the summer, we didn't see one another regularly, so it had been easy not to tell folks what was up. I looked into their smiling faces, and thought, "Well, hell, Cricket. Here's the flip side of passing as someone without cancer. Now you have to drop this bomb on them."

"Um, well, actually, I'm not getting my hair *cut*. . ." I said, nervously tucking my wig's perfect chin-length bob behind my ear. "Actually, um, I'm waiting for it to grow in. I had to do chemo all summer, and I've been wearing a wig since early July. . . ." I smiled at them awkwardly. They just stared. Then they erupted.

"Wha—?" "Are you kidding?" "That's not your hair?" "OMG, you have cancer?"

"I know, I know, it's crazy, but there you have it."

I stepped into the choir room, where we hung our robes tidily in large lockers, and then stepped back out into the hallway. One of my pals said, "Mirabelle's. Stat." This was code for us to find our way over to Burlington's sweet French bakery and café. Leunig's was for dreaming and soothing the soul. El Gato was for tequila and raging against the machine. Mirabelle's was for cups of strong French coffee and sharing secrets of the heart. Within ten minutes we were all around a table, and they were staring stunned at my suntanned face and glistening hair, only now noticing the missing eyebrows and eyelashes, and the puffiness from the steroids.

"So, tell all," Leigh said. And then there was silence. As I lowered my steaming cup, I could see Sally glancing at my button-down shirt. "No, no. I don't have breast cancer," I started. "It's non-Hodgkin's lymphoma, and it's almost gone, just one more round of chemo to go."

It was always hard to know just how to talk about it. If I used the jokes and props my family had created, calling my wig "Harriet" and laughing about not having to shave my legs all summer, well, some people weren't at all sure what to do with that information. The nurses had taught me about titration, slowly dripping the lethal stuff into a large amount of something innocuous, so as to dilute the impact and damage. So that's how I proceeded, amidst the croissants and hash browns and black coffee, explaining everything.

"I feel fine—honestly. I was out bicycling on the lakefront yesterday. Yes, this is a wig. Look closely, and I can show you the edge here over my ear. I know—it looks more real than my usual hair." I explained how the cancer was discovered, and how the summer had flown by.

"But wait," Kim questioned. "We were all in the choir that one Saturday in July, at Carol's funeral. You were there, and you were fine." I explained that was the very week my hair started to come out in clumps, how I'd had to ask my wig maker to deliver my new hair a few days early, because I wasn't comfortable going to the funeral knowing that I might have very noticeable gaps on my scalp. "That," I concluded, "was the very first day I wore the wig in public. I was terrified, and yet when I blended into the choir, I realized that nobody had noticed. That was the greatest gift you could have given me that day, not noticing."

We sipped in silence for a little while, chasing flakes of pastry around our plates, and shaking our heads in wonder at how life can take such sharp turns so fast. And then, just as I longed it would, the topic changed to someone else's teenager, and then on to another's garden disaster, and I relaxed into the lives and challenges they were facing, as my cancer became just one thing among many that we were dealing with as summer turned to fall.

WALKING THE SACRED PATH

You enter a maze to lose yourself. You enter a labyrinth to find yourself.

—traditional wisdom of the labyrinth

It was 5:00 pm when I parked in the lot at All Saints' Episcopal Church, in South Burlington. Their community labyrinth is tucked behind the church, and is approached by crossing a little wooden bridge. The symbolism of having to "cross over" to another place in order to approach the labyrinth resonated inside me. It reminded me that I wasn't just walking in circles around someone's backyard, but rather that I was leaving behind my day-to-day life, and entering into a liminal space, a place where the line between earthly and divine could blur. A "thin space," as the ancients would describe it, where the membrane between this world and the next might be more fluid, more permeable.

I had fallen ill the week after my fifth chemo round. Terrified as I was of getting an infection out in the world, I ironically picked up a cold that was going around in the oncology department at the hospital. Having canceled that month's pilgrimage due to a nagging fever, I found myself at loose ends until I remembered the labyrinths.

When medieval folks found that a pilgrimage was beyond their reach geographically, or financially, or physically, there was an alternative. Pilgrims would walk a labyrinth as a symbolic journey. The resurgence of popularity for labyrinths today means that one can often find a labyrinth not far from home. Retreat centers, churches, and even hospitals often have a public labyrinth to offer. It took me less than a minute on labyrinthlocator.com to find several within minutes of my apartment.

All Saints' labyrinth is built of bricks laid flush into the ground, probably to allow for easier mowing of the grassy paths and surrounding area. It is circled with comfortable benches, offering a seat for anyone wishing to contemplate the symmetrical paths without walking them. Someone had recently mowed, and the warm summer evening air smelled sweet and grassy. Approaching from the bridge, you almost don't see the labyrinth, so effortlessly does it blend into the lawn and scenery. I was nearly upon it before I made out its shape and orientation, locating the opening to the path.

Placing my car keys on one of the benches, I stood at the mouth of the path and paused. I closed my eyes, listening to the whir of insects and the occasional passing of cars on the road, and let myself sink inwards for a moment. My breathing slowed, and I recalled a quote from one of the pilgrimage books I'd recently read, saying that a pilgrim should not worry about a map. Just walk. *Just walk.*

Opening my eyes, I stepped onto the labyrinth, and felt immense joy. It is a sweet thing, to relax into ancient tradition. In my mind's eye, I felt myself connected spiritually with folks who might, at that very moment, be walking the famous labyrinths at Grace Cathedral in San Francisco, or at Chartres Cathedral in France. Somewhere on the earth, others walked before and behind me, walked even beside me through the first turn of the labyrinth. I felt my heart connect through time to those who had traveled great distances to make their pilgrimage labyrinth journey, thousands of years before the Common Era.

Looking at a labyrinth pattern, you may notice a resemblance to the brain, as the archetypal image seems familiar even the first time you see it. Long before recorded history, these circular paths and parallel circuits were etched on cave walls, to be found by others in an unimaginable future. The most famous labyrinth was the one designed by Daedalus for King Minos at his palace complex of Knossos on the island of Crete. Coins produced four hundred years before the Common Era on Crete were inscribed with the single-circuit design that is known today, showing an early understanding of a labyrinth as being distinct from a maze. A maze lures you into cul-de-sacs and confusing backtracks, but a labyrinth is one path, which you follow as it loops and circles its way to the center.

A labyrinth walk for me is a way to let go of grasping, let go of accomplishing, let go of a goal. The path in this labyrinth suddenly swung toward the very center after just a few turns, making me unconsciously think I was heading for the center spot, before swinging far and away again around the periphery. It's a reminder to enjoy the journey. This moment is all that we have.

Just as it does in meditation, my mind wandered while walking, one moment feeling nothing other than the grass under my feet, and the next instant praying in gratitude for the many friends and family members and health professionals who were keeping me alive with their work and love; then suddenly I'd find myself thinking about what I'd have for dinner, and in the next moment remembering that I had to do laundry later. What I love about the labyrinth is the swinging to right and left, the U-turns, the long straight stretches before another series of turns. No hurry, no goal, no "should" or "must." Just the next step, the next step, the next step.

I became lost in a dream about the chemo journey, thinking about how there are no choices in a labyrinth; you simply walk it through to the end. There are no side roads, no escape routes, no shortcuts. Like a sharp piercing of my heart, I heard again in my imagination my anger, fear, sorrow, and fighting over the change of chemo regimen.

In one defiant moment earlier that month, when my doctor was on vacation and his colleague had seen me and recommended radiation following the chemo, I had actually said, "I'll just decline radiation. I think if it comes to that, I'll just say no." Tears sprang into my eyes. I knew on some level that this choice was not mine. Like the labyrinth, I had to walk the entire path, and not just the sections I chose. Did I want to find myself needing chemo again? Did I want to fight this battle without using all the possible artillery available? If a medical professional made a recommendation for my healing, was my amateur intellect worth a darn in that conversation? I didn't know how to cure cancer. My job was to believe, to trust, to pray, and to walk.

Earlier that month, I had stayed up all night watching the movie *The Way*. In it, a father walks the *camino*, or pilgrimage road, to Santiago de Compostela in Spain, as a memorial to his lost son. I was smitten, and overflowed with newfound passion to go on that pilgrimage, to spend five or six weeks walking over the Pyrenees from France, through the streets of Pamplona where my brother had several times run with the bulls, sleeping in rough hostels and sharing meals and conversation with pilgrims from around the world. To me, this sounds like heaven. In that week's therapy session, Max had just shaken his head. "Why not go to Spain on vacation, and just enjoy yourself? Does everything for you have to turn into an epic challenge?" Huh. You mean walking eight hundred miles doesn't sound like fun? Don't confuse me with the facts—that I really don't much like walking in the first place, or that if I had second thoughts each time I went to spend two or three days at a monastery, how on earth would I feel the morning I awoke to face down that eight-hundred-mile journey?

Looping my way deeper into the labyrinth, my mind shifted to the *camino*, and walking those hundreds of miles to Santiago de Compostela. The pilgrim's journey isn't over when he or she tires of it. It isn't over when the going gets hard, or the weather gets bad. It isn't over when you're bored or homesick.

Your pilgrimage place might be a holy site, or it might be your grandparents' home, or Graceland, or all of the national parks or baseball stadiums in the country. Your *goal* is what you think will be important but it turns out that the *journey*, from the planning to the execution of the plan, is where your dreams and energy will take wing. The labyrinth walk can be a metaphor, with your imagined goal in the center: Jerusalem, Mecca, God, healing, freedom from addiction, peace. You can imagine the walk toward the center as a time to cast off old, outgrown thoughts or choices. Having reached the center, you then turn around and walk outward, holding yourself open to new life and directions. I have heard it said that the labyrinth includes an equal number of right- and left-handed turns, so as to "balance the humors" of the brain and achieve physiological balance in the body. True or not, I feel like my whole body is spun and centered through the walking.

The labyrinth that evening was sheer magic. So many worries and loose ends that had been jangling around in my head and my heart for weeks found some kind of resolution that night. They were resolved not because I thought about them, but rather because I did *not* think about them, and somehow the peace that I needed in my spirit to find solutions or resolutions only bubbled up to the surface when I actively let them go.

Tradition translates Compostela as "field of stars," and I thought of that as I found myself suddenly in the center of the labyrinth and saw the stars beginning to shine in the still-light September sky. We each walk our path until we find ourselves in the field of stars. I knew I would have to stay open and walk wherever the path of the cancer treatment would lead me, just as that lovely night I would walk the entire labyrinth once, twice, and then a third time for luck.

CHEMO ROUND SIX

Round *six*.

Every single day, for fifteen weeks, as soon as my eyes opened I had reached for a pad of paper by my bed and recorded my resting pulse rate and taken my temperature. I had ambled into the bathroom and brushed my teeth, without looking in the mirror at my scratchy, sore scalp, and pulled on Harriet the Wig before I even put on my eyeglasses. I had, throughout each day, tracked my bathroom habits as if they were celestial signs. Just before my first day of chemo, I had written out on that pad the date for every day for eighteen weeks, so I could watch as the days, then weeks, then months ticked by. This morning I turned to the final page, the final week, the final round of chemo.

This was the only round that had "opening ceremonies" the entire weekend beforehand. My mom came to visit, so I drove down to meet up with her and Tom, at our house in New Hampshire. We spent Saturday driving around on dirt roads for the annual Wool Arts Farm Tour. Fiber farms, which raised anything from Angora bunnies to alpacas and sheep, opened for the entire weekend, and each hosted booths from a number of local yarn and weaving and spinning shops as well. Blissfully we drove through the bright fall foliage, each farm offering something unique and the camaraderie at all of them lively and joyful.

That night, a few friends joined us for a small dinner party. Seeing their faces, and letting them see that I was feeling well and strong, was deeply healing. Moving away from these people I loved had been brutal, and there was great healing in hearing their voices and laughter. I felt strong, and loved, and ready for the last round.

The next morning, Tom and Mom and I drove up to Vermont, stopping in Montpelier to have Sunday brunch at the New England Culinary Institute. We made a day out of it, wandering around Burlington's shops and celebrating the beginning of The Final Round.

The silver lining of the Satchel of Death was that I didn't have a ten-hour day at the hospital on Monday. After about half the day, I was hooked up to the travel IV and released. Mom, Tom, and I wandered around town some more, enjoying the lakefront, the fall foliage, and finding a spot for another celebratory dinner. In the morning, Tom and Mom headed back to New Hampshire, where he put her on her flight back to Virginia before heading back to work himself.

I was feeling some nervousness about the week, because I had to be on a plane myself on Friday afternoon, heading to Pennsylvania to perform another wedding. Jan, mother of the groom, was my Cellmate whose retirement from the Pentagon in June had been the occasion around which my knitting siblings had gathered and worked so hard to surprise me with the Magic Shawl. Missing that long-awaited gathering had been heartbreaking, so I was desperate not to disappoint for this event. I was very anxious that the chemo run as planned, and that I would be released in plenty of time to get to the airport and be there for the rehearsal on Friday night.

Nevertheless, there were celebrations to be had, even in the infusion suite. On Friday, as the nurses disconnected the IV for the final time, a bell was rolled in for me to ring to my heart's content as a signal that I was now done with chemo. I complied, adding a brief Highland fling as well, prompting the fellow receiving chemo across from me to perform a wild pole dance with his IV pole, much to the mixed horror and delight of the onlookers. My nurses gathered around to hug me and wish me well, and by the end we all were wiping tears from our eyes. In the presence of illness and fear, we had also shared a great deal of laughter and joy. We had woven our lives together pretty tightly since June. Now the fabric was being cut in two.

As I looked around at their smiles and tears, it struck me how brave these women were. For me, chemo was eighteen weeks, but for them it was every single day. My chair would be filled the next week with a new cancer, a new chart, a new face, and that person would then begin to build a new relationship with these same nurses. They opened themselves and their lives and hearts to each one of us, caring for us, bonding with us, and then having to let us go, sometimes to life and sometimes to death. And yet, they kept on, remaining open and gentle, when hardening or distancing themselves from other people's pain and fear would have been understandable. At the end, the tenderness I felt for them overwhelmed me.

But, no dallying—off to the airport.

Jan's twin sister Ellen, another of my knitting Cellmates, was meeting me at the airport. I was so happy to see her I cried, and then she cried, and then when we dried our tears I noticed another impossible, universe-affirming coincidence. Since the Cellmates are all avid knitters, we were passionate about each other's knitwear. With the explosion of online knitting communities and the availability of patterns on websites such as Ravelry,[21] one of us always had something astonishing to show or teach the others, every time we gathered. So, wiping tears away, I looked at Ellen's sweater. I couldn't believe it. It was the exact same sweater that I had been knitting on the plane. Tens of thousands of sweater patterns out there, and I was knitting the same one she was wearing on the afternoon she picked me up at

---

21. I just searched for "sweater patterns" on Ravelry.com, and up came over 86,000 patterns.

the airport? Thank you, Universe, for affirming that we were indeed separated at birth. Well, of course, she had actually been born as Jan's twin. I was like a long-distance triplet, really.

We hopped into the rental car, and headed west, into Amish country. Rural Pennsylvania's rolling hills were lovely in the fading light, and Ellen and I talked wildly, catching up on the cancer, the chemo, her family, the wedding guests, and of course, our knitting.

"Oh, are you staying at Jan's?" I asked. "I know I'm staying at some B&B that Jan said was nearby."

Ellen looked over at me. "Then Jan didn't tell you?" She raised one eyebrow slightly, registering her surprise.

"Um, no. But hey, I'm cool anywhere. I take so many drugs right now, day and night are all the same to me. I had my last huge predni-sone dose today, and when it's bedtime, I'll pop the downer drug, and it'll be lights out. What was she going to tell me?"

I pause for a moment to remind you, gentle reader, that Jan had been an admiral in the Navy, serving in ways that were unimaginable to me. Ellen started to laugh. "Oh Cricket—never let someone who has lived in a cargo container in Baghdad book you a room. Yes, you and I are in the same B&B. Better than that, we're in the same room. Not only that, we're in the same bed." With this she dissolved in laughter, while I waited for the punch line. Gasping between giggles, she said, "The room has a king-size bed. In Jan's mind, that is enough sleeping space for, who knows? Five or six people at least. We'll have to wait to see if anyone else joins us in there." We laughed till even more tears ran down our cheeks. How good, how very good, to have this weekend together.

It was chilly and dark when we got to the farm. Oh, I forgot to mention that Jan and her husband Dale had bought a farm. So Jan could, you know, raise alpacas and sheep (I *told* you we took our knit-ting seriously). The wedding couple was in high spirits, and the house and yard rang with merriment. Nevertheless, I could feel the heavy tiredness of the chemo day, the flight, and the trip beginning to take a

toll as we rehearsed the brief outdoor ceremony in the chill of the evening. Then, everyone draped themselves over furniture in the house
while we noshed and heard about the next day's battle plan. When the
groom's parents are career Army and career Navy, trust me, there's a
battle plan.

Sometime in the evening, I remembered my package of syringes.
"Oh, Jan? Is there a corner of the fridge where I could stash my drugs?"
She smiled. "Of course. Look here, there's nothing in this butter com-
partment. Will they fit here?" They did, and so there was nothing left
but to party and celebrate this final chemo day, ending with whis-
pers and giggles in the king-size bed like fifth graders at a sleepover.
Thankfully, nobody else joined us.

RHINEBECK

A foolish consistency is the hobgoblin of small minds . . . Speak what you think now in hard words, and to-morrow speak what to-morrow thinks in hard words again, though it contradict every thing you said to-day.

—Ralph Waldo Emerson

When my full treatment plan had been explained to me, I felt sincere pleasure at the timing of things. Summer, my least favorite season, would be spent in hospitals. I was happy to think of all that free air-conditioning. Fall, my favorite season, would see the end of treatment and my return to full health and activity. What joy to awaken on that crisp October day when this all would be over!

My final chemo round and the quick trip to Pennsylvania for the wedding were followed by one of the year's greatest weekends for knitters, the Dutchess County Sheep and Wool Festival. Perfectly timed, my knitting Cellmates from around the country were primed for the twofold celebration of "Rhinebeck" (as the festival is known, since it's held in Rhinebeck, NY) and the end of my chemo. And so, pilgrimage six would be a trip to a festival and not a monastery. I was cool with that.

The original three of us, Ellen, Joan, and I, had drawn in family and other friends to join the group, and we now included friends from southern California, Chicago, and upstate Minnesota as well. So many of us were gathering at Rhinebeck that we ended up renting two neighboring cabins deep in the New York countryside, where we could plot our course through several days of knitting and spinning classes, celebratory meals, drool-worthy "show & tell" sessions after binge-buying in the marketplaces, and of course idyllic evenings knitting and spinning and talking late into the night. Never in my dearest dreams could I have imagined ending my chemo and cancer journey with a more perfect gathering.

I had asked my nurse Kristen if a massive sheep and wool festival would be safe for me, just a few days after my final chemo round. She had watched me knit my way through many a long chemo day, and knew my passion for all things fiber. I dreaded thinking that she might ask me to wear a yellow surgical mask the whole time, something that, on top of the wig, seemed like the ultimate embarrassment. "Well," she prevaricated, "I don't know. Exactly what do you imagine doing there?" I excitedly told her of the pens of prize Merinos, the handsome Roman noses of the Bluefaced Leicesters, the cages filled with Angora bunnies, and the wavy locks of the cashmere goats. And of course, the sheepdog demonstrations, the crazy food booths, the marketplace stretching out through dozens of barns, and all tied together by the fluty music of a Peruvian band. "Hmm. . . OK," she said, "Under one condition. Don't lick any llamas, all right?" She stared at me perfectly seriously, and then we both burst out laughing. I thought that, with some restraint, I could probably follow her restriction.

There was much rejoicing as I collected a few Cellies at the airport in Vermont, stopped by the hospital for my second blood draw of the week, and then drove across to New York to find and settle into our cabins. From hither and yon, we arrived by car, plane, and train. The excitement was palpable.

And yet.

And yet, there was *something*. A canker sore, I supposed, was forming on the side of my tongue. You know how annoying those are, bumping into your teeth and causing a little wince of pain? As Deb and Karen and I drove through the afternoon sunshine, I could feel it cropping up, strangely more sore than any other canker sore of my life. Still, a trivial thing. No big deal, right?

Except, well, a few more miles along, I felt a growing soreness on the floor of my mouth under my tongue, and a sprouting sore there, and then within minutes another sore on the underside of my tongue. And at the back of my throat. And then the other side of my tongue. Like a time-lapse video, I could feel ten or more separate open ulcers emerging from the depths of my mouth and tongue. Driving to this wonderful weekend, I found myself squinting with pain and fear as my heart raced. What was happening in my mouth? What on earth was happening to me?

Later, after all of this, I would learn that my doctor, determined that the final chemo round would kill off that stubborn glowing crescent inside me, had increased my dose for this final round. Perhaps someone was meant to have told me to keep an eye out for increased side effects? Nevertheless, throughout my treatment, I had thanked God that I felt mostly all right. Looking around the chemo suite was all the reminder I needed that chemo brings intense suffering to many people. I knew there was a thin line between their experience and my own, and that at any moment the scales could tip. After having become accustomed first to the original treatment and then to the more rigorous Satchel of Death drugs, the aftermath of round six of my chemo was unlike anything else I'd experienced. I don't know if anticipating the changes would have helped, but the pain and shock of my mouth erupting in open sores was intense, especially as I was so primed to celebrate the happy ending of my treatment all weekend.

By the time we got to the cabins, breathing was excruciating. Swallowing? Insane. Even my speech was slurred, as I tried to navigate my tongue in my mouth without any surfaces touching, an impossibility. The joy of seeing my friends made me shy to admit I was suffering so much, and so I sipped tiny breaths of air, and tried like hell to get my mind out of my mouth and disconnected from the pain. Had I been alone, would meditation have helped? I have no idea. I would certainly have run to the hospital with my tail between my legs, crying uncle. Later I would learn of a prescription mixture of Lidocaine and Benadryl, called "Magic Mouthwash," which is some- times useful for these sores. I would also learn that the pain of these sores sometimes could only be managed with intravenous morphine, in the hospital. It was a whole new level of hurt for me.

We gathered at a diner to kick off the evening. For the most part, I could distract myself with their laughing banter, though I kept my own mouth uncharacteristically closed for more of the time than usual. There was much talk of the wedding weekend some of us had just enjoyed, and others checked in with their recent adventures. Eyeballing the menu, I ordered the mac and cheese, thinking that its softness in my mouth would be bearable, and that perhaps the dairy would coat my tongue and lessen the pain. No dice. I couldn't even chew, though I was hungry. Gently I forked one macaroni at a time into my mouth, swallowing them whole. Looking around the table at my best friends, my heart swelled and I vowed not to bring them down. I planned a pharmacy stop on the way back to the cabins, with the thought of loading up with ibuprofen and Chloraseptic mouth spray. It would be all right. I could get through this as I had every- thing else.

Fistfuls of ibuprofen allowed me to fall into a much-needed, deep sleep, though the Chloraseptic didn't begin to numb the mouth pain. Trying gently to eat a glazed doughnut the next morning startled me with how sharp tiny edges of sugar can be. I worked at gum- ming down a few bites, and then turned back to my coffee. With my sense of smell AWOL anyway, I wasn't missing much skipping meals. As everyone got ready for the day, I slid one of my syringes out of the fridge and plunged it into my stomach. That morning, the now routine sting of the beveled needle was among the least of my worries. Funny how everything is relative.

The festival *was* glorious. Crowds of people, a beautiful autumn day, miles to walk while groping our way through fleeces, yarn booths, animal pens (no licking), classes, and demos. For the most part, I could ignore my mouth and focus on being surrounded by the goodness of my friends. I practiced breathing through my nose in a way that kept most of the air moving along the back of my throat and not across my tongue. Midway through the day, hours before our official time to regroup, I felt my energy flag, so I slid off back into the vast parking area, and let myself into the car. Swallowing down another large fistful of ibuprofen and tipping the driver's seat back, I fell into a deep sleep for several hours. Awaking considerably refreshed, I wandered back into the fray and found some of my friends, and we enjoyed the final hours of the festival.

That night, after dinner in a friendly pub (where I *may* have self-medicated with some local beer, just a wee bit), and after our circle time of show & tell, I quietly explained my mouth sores to Karen, the doctor among us (she had been indispensable to me before round one by sharing her wise counsel on the maintenance of bowels during chemo). She confirmed, with deep compassion, that this was indeed a chemo side effect, though we were both mystified at why it had only happened this one time. I was relieved that, although my tongue and mouth were still miserably sore on all of their surfaces, no new sores had appeared, and a few of the smaller ones seemed to be resolving. This too would pass, and I relaxed into the thought that since this had been the final chemo round, the worst was over.

In so many ways, this was true. And in one big way, it was not.

Two weeks after Rhinebeck, I had my final PET scan, to give me the all clear, and prove that my treatment had come to an end. But that's not what happened.

RADIATION

The heart is otherwise unremarkable.

—observation from my PET scan

The truth is, I don't think I had anything against radiation, before I started chemo. However, I didn't understand the behind-the-scenes geekiness of doctors. At some point in med school, they had to pick their specialties, and most remain fiercely loyal to that choice. Medical school is like Hogwarts: some are drawn to Spells, others to Herbology, and still others to Potions. My oncologist was Potions, all the way. To him, radiation was a suspicious combination of Spells and Defense Against the Dark Arts.

At one of our initial visits, he had said, "Because of your age, I'd prefer not to have to do radiation." When I laughed and told him I wasn't all that old, he smiled and added, "I meant, patients as *young* as you. Radiation has, among its side effects, the possibility of causing other cancers down the road: breast, throat, thyroid, lung, not to mention heart damage. . . . The younger you are, the more years you have for something like that to crop up. In any event, I think we'll be able to skip radiation in your case, altogether."

Since that was my doctor's spin on treatment, I became "anti-radiation" myself. I mean, seriously? It might cause more cancers? No thank you. One was more than enough.

When my final PET scan results came back. I was not worried. Since there had just been that one thin shimmer of light still visible along the edge of the tumor at the halfway point, we were all pretty confident that the cancer would show itself to be well and truly beaten. I had been told that a chemo-resistant version of NHL would be bad news, that if the cancer wasn't gone after one full round of chemo the follow-up options had dramatically worse survival statistics. Basically, I'd been told that if the tumor wasn't dead, I was screwed.

The tumor was not dead. Or, well, maybe it was. . . the doctors couldn't tell. They couldn't read the scan. Something wasn't right. The PET scan after six rounds of chemo looked *precisely* like the PET scan after three rounds. Was it still cancer? Was something unrelated showing up on the scan? Was it just inflammation from the treatment? Or, as my family assumed, did they mix up the scans? Were they looking at the wrong one?

My friends, family, and long email list of people in my support network were all hovering by their phones or email, to hear good news. Meanwhile, I was staring at Gianni with my face frozen in place. Oh crap. This was seriously not good news. The report said:

There is a stable appearance to the right anterior mediastinal mass with no significant change in the FDG-uptake.

"Stable" is not a good word here. Stable meant unchanged. It meant chemo-resistant. It meant death. Somewhere deep inside me, my confidence and joy at having finished chemo evaporated. Meanwhile, Gianni seemed. . . what? Sad? Angry? Disappointed? Looking at his apologetic expression, I felt that I had let him down. After all his hard work, how could I have failed him like this?

He went on to tell me that he was meeting with the radiation team to see if I could "benefit from their services." He looked embarrassed and defeated, in an unreadable sort of way. Meanwhile, my head was spinning, trying to absorb this information. One, the PET scan didn't look good. Two, he was now talking radiation. . . but didn't he say that would cause more cancers?

Gianni murmured something about calling me on the phone, and checking in, and an appointment as soon as possible to talk with the doctors over there, and then I was out of the office and down the hall, and in the car. I had to go home, to the computer, and write some kind of note to my Prayer Warriors. . . only, I didn't have a clue what to say.

The road to equanimity is not a smooth one. As Dr. Arnie Kozak says on his "Mindfulness Matters" blog, describing his concept of Equanimity Equity: "The more we practice [mindful meditation], the more equanimity we have in the bank."[22] Basically, this news bankrupted my account, and left me high and dry, overreacting, lashing out, shutting down. All my newly honed coping skills evaporated.

I had worked so hard to get through my planned eighteen weeks of treatment in one piece. It felt as though all of the spiritual work I'd done, learning to be curious, learning not to react but respond, learning to accept news without labeling, learning not to play out dramatic future storylines, learning to live more in the moment. . . all of this failed me.

Of course, I could have predicted this, if I hadn't been myself in the center of it. No spiritual journey is a straight line. Often the path turns, we lose our way, we feel that all is lost, we retrace our steps and curse the darkness or the light or whatever we think is the problem. Looking back now, I am struck by how my emails reflect, *in order*, Elisabeth Kübler-Ross's classic stages of grief.

---

22. Dr. Arnie Kozak, "Check the Balance of Your Equanimity Equality," Mindfulness Matters, http://www.beliefnet.com/columnists/mindfulnessmatters/2016/03/check-the-balance-of-your-equanimity-equity.html.

Stage one, Denial: The day Gianni first showed me the PET results, I wrote this to my mom:

> I got totally neutral news from the doc. It seems like this week's PET looks just like the one from the halfway point . . .
>
> The doc says the mediastinal area is notoriously tricky to read, so he's going to go chat with the radiology docs about it. I'll chat with him again Mon or Tues. Most likely is I'll have another needle biopsy to double check that what is lighting up is really just necrotic tissue or something else unrelated to the lymphoma.
>
> Less happy scenario, he'll recommend radiation or more chemo, but I honestly don't think we're going there. I think the biopsy will clear me . . . I'm really not worried.

I especially love how I keep calling the doctors' conversations "chats," instead of life-or-death treatment decisions.

Stage two, Anger: Six days later, I was railing in an email to my friend Chris, sounding like a furious toddler (well, a furious toddler with a penchant for profanity):

> Last week's PET scan showed that the cancer is not gone. Now I have to meet with radiology, even though we had hoped to avoid that. Aiming radiation straight into the thoracic cavity has a solid track record of causing heart damage, as well as breast/throat/lung/and/or bone cancer down the road.
>
> fuck fuck fuckity fuck.
>
> I had the healing service today at noon at the Cathedral and sweet folks surrounded me with healing and love, which helped a lot. . . but I'm really pissed off about this. . . . [cue mid-rant shift to stage three, Bargaining] . . . I was a good girl and did all that chemo, with the understanding that I'd be cured. . . and the fact that I'm not, and now have to do this really dangerous next

step, is making me incoherent with [shifting again, now to stage four, Depression] angry/sad/helplessness. It's coming in waves, and I have to suck it down. . . . But I am rage rage raging about it. I'm even pissed at my therapist, for no particular reason.

. . . The information about all of this has been coming in fast, and each time I heard it wrong or differently, so only yesterday did it all hit the fan when my oncologist called to give me the lowdown. Up until then, I was still in denial.

And then, finally, a full week after the news, I actually watched my brain shift into stage five, Acceptance, when I wrote to my nurse asking for a copy of the PET scan:

Since I'll be with family all next week for Thanksgiving, I'm thinking we could use it for a rousing game of darts. . . . or maybe "pin the radiation beam on the tumor". . . . This is good, Kristen. My sense of humor is coming back.

~~~~~~

Toward the end of my chemo, I went looking for a new massage therapist. I've long been a believer in the deep healing power of massage on emotional and psychological levels, as well as the physical. As the cancer journey drew to a close, I wanted to start rebuilding my health on all these levels, and massage seemed like one sure way to help. It did occur to me that massage moves the lymph around in the body, and I wasn't sure if that was a good idea during lymphoma treatment. However, my doctor said it would be fine, so I went strolling through the internet to find a good match for a new therapist.

Burlington is a community with a real appreciation for healing and bodywork, so there were dozens of massage therapists and other bodywork professionals to consider. As happened over and over again in these months, the person I most needed to meet at that point in my journey fell right into place when I went looking. Darren's biography jumped off the screen at me:

> Darren treats all individuals seeking the benefits of physical, mental, emotional and spiritual wellness. . . . He also specializes in working with clients with chronic pain, illness and injury including cancer, depression, stroke, cerebral palsy, and multiple sclerosis. . . . He is deeply committed to an ongoing meditation practice and believes in the benefits of quieting one's mind in order to assist in healing and wellness.

A massage therapist with his own meditation practice. One who specialized in treating cancer patients, and those seeking "spiritual wellness"? There were dozens of others to choose among, but this was clearly where the Spirit was leading me. As my own meditation practice was developing, I found myself encountering others on the path who encouraged in me the same things I was working on, and modeled ways of living mindfully in the world and through their vocations. As it turned out, I was to learn and receive much from Darren.

My first appointment was for a standard massage. Like all good therapists, he spent time first asking about my life, getting to know my health, asking questions, and listening deeply. When I found out he was also a lymphoma survivor, my heart leapt. During my treatment months, the thing that gave me the most hope was meeting survivors, and daring to imagine that I would become one myself.

He spoke compassionately and honestly of his own journey, the fears and setbacks that inevitably are a part of the path. He asked precisely the right questions about me and my cancer, veering more toward questions about my relationship with my treatment, and where my head was in the middle of all that was happening. He completely understood how a cancer diagnosis leads to a sense that you have been betrayed by your body, and how hard it is to trust it again. With our common cancer bond, I found I could easily be honest with him about some of the dark places inside me that weren't aired anywhere else. Clearly this wasn't just going to be about massage. It was a place for me to continue to learn about being vulnerable, to learn to accept healing into those deepest, darkest places.

Darren's specialty is something called myofascial release.[23] This treatment targets the fascia, which might be imagined as an interior sweater of connective tissue that completely enrobes your body, under the skin but over your muscles. I knew that a fascial sheath covers a muscle, but it never occurred to me that the layer doesn't just cover individual body parts—it connects them all.[24] Probably the best-known section is on the sole of the foot, known when injured as plantar fasciitis. Treatments for that often target just the foot, but the ongoing cause of that injury may actually be from somewhere else in the body, where the fascia is pulling, tightening, or otherwise compromised. Myofascial release (MFR) aims to identify areas in the body where that connective tissue may have become habitually tight, and release it so that all parts of the body can enjoy easy movement and suppleness in their relationship with one another. At a time when I desperately wanted to befriend my body again and live in harmony with it, MFR sounded like a perfect fit.

My first MFR session, a few weeks later, was scheduled right between Gianni's referring me to the radiation department and my first appointment with them. I was in a tailspin of fear and fright, and angry that the treatment weeks I had so carefully counted down were now extended indefinitely. My rant, which I'd rehearsed in my email to Chris, centered on spouting half-learned and inflated details about all the dangers of radiation. During our check-in, Darren listened patiently as I railed about the injustice of it all. My main fear was that the radiation could cause other cancers in the future. How could I

---

23. He was a student of John F. Barnes, and offers that "lineage" of MFR.
24. In a visual, but somewhat gross illustration, you have encountered the fascia if you have ever removed "silverskin" from the surface of a piece of meat you were about to cook.

choose a treatment plan now that might turn around and kill me in another few years? What if I survived the cancer only to discover the radiation had caused untreatable damage to my heart? Caught in a negative-feedback loop, I kept hammering away at my argument, and spinning myself into a sad, angry place.

Finally, I ran out of steam. We sat in silence for a moment or two, all of my sorrow and fear hanging in the air around us. With infinite tenderness, Darren leaned forward and said, "And, how is this working for you?" Confused, I asked what he meant. "This," he continued, "this fighting and resisting? How is it making you feel?"

Not quite getting his point, I launched back into a laundry list of how rotten I felt, how angry, how let down. And again, only when I had fully unloaded and fallen silent, he asked again. "This way of receiving this news. How is it making you feel? Yes, of course you are in a frightening place, and your concerns are valid. But you get to decide how to accept the information, and how to move forward. Two weeks ago you told me you were feeling stronger and healthier every day. Don't let this news affect how well you were feeling."

(Insert sound of Chinese gong here.)

Could it be that I'd once again forgotten everything I'd been working so hard to learn? How had I completely forgotten the "wisdom of no escape"? The diagnostic news wasn't making me crazy, the unpredictability of the cancer and its treatment wasn't making me crazy. *I* was making me crazy through this resisting, this fighting. I reminded myself, "Suffering is the distance between the truth of this present reality and what we wish it were." How vastly I had increased my suffering in these weeks between chemo and radiation. Oh my God. Once again, cancer was not the cause of my suffering. I was.

Like a whack with the Stick of Compassion, Darren's question was all I needed to reboot. It would take some time to get my mind and body aligned again, but he broke the cycle by reminding me I could step out of it whenever I was ready.

On to the treatment.

Talking about my experience of MFR is like talking about how I felt when I grew roots in the church at New Skete. It was startling and mystical. The actual treatment is not shockingly unusual. If anything, it is like very slow-motion massage, involving deep static holds followed by strong, slowly shifting pressure. For reasons I can't explain, it released a deluge of images within my brain, images of strength, of health, of power.

For instance, in the very first session he began by holding onto my shins, just holding them where they were as my legs rested along the table. After a stretch of time, he began slowly to shake them, first subtly and then with more strength, shaking my shins back and forth.

In my mind's eye, it was as though I were a sculpture, a piece of art, that had been covered over in mud and left hidden. As he shook me, I could feel the dark, ugly mud begin to crack all over the surface of my body, and then fall in great chunks to the table and floor. Something in me was being uncovered, allowed to emerge.

Next, he placed his hands on my knees, and repeated the pressure and then the rocking. A vision arose of all the times I've knelt in prayer, the pressure on my knees like the instant replay of every time I'd found myself kneeling, as a priest or long ago as a child. The pressure felt as if all the prayers I'd ever prayed were being released and lifted up again.

He moved to my head, cradling it, then gently rocking it back and forth. Other than the monks and nuns of Zen Mountain Monastery, Darren was the only person who ever saw me without my wig. Having my bald head gently manipulated felt like being born, being drawn with gentleness out of this holding pattern and into a new beginning.

Lastly, he pressed one hand down on my sternum and held.

In a lightning-bolt moment, I realized that the cause of all of this, the central character of this entire drama—that original thymic neoplasm—lived directly under my breastbone, but that in all of these six months *not one single person had touched me in that place.* I'd been poked and probed, I'd been biopsied and scanned, but then they looked at the scans, the numbers, the reports. As Darren's hand applied pressure, it felt to me as though the pressure became a golden, healing light streaming at last, after all of this poisonous treatment, right into my chest cavity and scattering the darkness of the cancer, and of my anxious thoughts.

As that warm light filled me, as his hand rested an inch above my dying tumor, I felt tears of healing acceptance and peace fill my closed eyes and roll sideways down to the table. I'd turned a corner. I was ready to move ahead.

Six days after Thanksgiving, I went over to the radiation department to meet with one of their doctors for the first time.

The hematology/oncology waiting room had been small, bleak, and cramped, rows of chairs jammed into too small a space. There were times I waited over two hours for a five-minute blood draw, when things got really backed up. (And I'm not complaining; you were seen fast when things went wrong. A long wait was a sign that you, and your cancer, were a lower priority than someone else's. Waiting was a good thing.)

The hallway to radiation had an arch over it, emblazoned with the promising words "Garden Pavilion." I paused under the arch, pulled out my phone, and asked a passerby to take my photo. It was like having my picture taken on the first day of school, though I couldn't say whether I had flunked out of the old school, or simply transferred to this new one. I just knew I was starting over again.

Then I walked through the doors of the radiation department, and stopped in my tracks. The waiting room stretched out like the lobby of a luxury hotel. There were conversation nooks with comfy loveseats upholstered with soft fabrics, tall potted palms, and wide open space with colors only a decorator specializing in tranquility could have imagined. It was gorgeous.

Here I had been raging against God and everyone else for a month, and half a second after I finally walked into the department, I never wanted to leave. The women behind the check-in desk were not wearing the usual scrubs, but rather had matching French blue polo shirts bearing the name of the department, and their logo: an Adirondack chair. What the hell had I been doing down the hall all these months? This was like a trip to the spa.

I had done my homework, and looked up the doctor I had been assigned on the internet. I could see her photo on the hospital website, and she looked a tad like a brilliant, mad scientist, her wildly curly hair and her sideways smile standing out among the other doctors. Googling her name, I discovered that she was on the *U.S. News and World Report's* "Top Doctors" list for 2012–2013. She had just been rated in the top 1 percent for excellence in radiation oncology. Once again, the puzzle pieces all slipped into place deep inside me. I wasn't just in good hands; I was in the best hands.

Having spent six months befriending and bonding with the doctors and nurses down the hall, I was nervous starting from scratch, but when the doctor bustled into the room grinning and holding out her hand, I was immediately charmed. Had we met in a different setting, we might have been pals, I think. She was funny, serious, smart, and able to shift from a sincere pastoral concern about me and my disease to a clinical explanation of the treatment she was recommending; I loved her compassion as well as her competence.

She too had done her homework. I thought our conversation was to be theoretical, as in "What does your PET scan look like, and what thoughts do I have about it?" Oh no. She had computer-generated images of my tumor on her desktop monitor, and delightedly showed me the large gray mass that was no longer alive, as well as the glimmering shadow along the edge. Zooming in, she then hit a button and the glimmer became a topographical map, with what looked like elevation circles flowing out from a center crescent. She had designed a treatment plan that, she smiled confidently at me, would completely eradicate what was left of the tumor while causing almost no collateral damage. "See?" she said intensely, leaning over her desk to stab her finger at the rings of varied radiation doses. "Look—I can stay away from your heart. This IMRT is very localized. We'll get all the bad cells, but not hurt too many of the healthy ones." A week earlier, I would have fixed her with a disbelieving gaze, but her smile and certainty completely disarmed me. Ten minutes after meeting her, I would have let that woman slice me open with a butter knife and shine a flashlight into the wound if she had told me it would work.

She led me into the next room, and I thought I was being prepped for a quick medical exam. Imagine my surprise when a perky nurse with a syringe mentioned casually that she would be my tattoo artist.

This was all moving too fast. What? I was being tattooed? This was a go?

What I had thought was a radiation consult was actually my prepping appointment for the beginning of treatment. The doctor's smile only flagged once, when she looked at my chart and asked why it had taken over a month for me to be referred to the department. Hmm. No idea. It's not like I was resisting this or anything. . .

I believe in signs. Throughout my treatment, I saw signs that encouraged me. I know that you can read almost anything into almost anything, but still, I believe. I watch and look for moments of serendipity, moments when it seems like the universe is yelling a great big "We got this" in my general direction.

Actually, these moments happen so often it's a wonder we don't trip over them. I got two signs in the weeks before radiation.

The first Sunday after I acknowledged I was going for radiation, I found myself at the altar, offering up the words of the collect, or special prayer, for the day:

Almighty God, give us grace to cast away the works of darkness,
and put on the armor of light . . .[25]

It was the first Sunday in the season of Advent, a season of prepa-
ration and anticipation. As the words came out of my mouth, I was
stunned. In this season of light, in the darkest time of year when
many faiths celebrated the gift of light, I was having a treatment that
was basically the aiming of light at my cancer. I was in fact putting on
the armor of light. That was all radiation was: my new armor to fight
with. Suddenly, the timing and the treatment were exactly right. I was
ready to cast away the works of darkness.

I prepared for my radiation by obsessing over a new playlist for
the sessions. The nurse had thought it would be all right to take my
iPhone into the treatment room, and so I pored over my tunes looking for something that would bolster my morale. I'd already used
The Firm's terrific "I'm Radioactive" as my jam for PET scans, though
when they saw my earbuds they made me stop, since listening to
music, talking, sitting up, even being in a well-lit room all were for-
bidden for ninety minutes before the scan. Basically, anything that
made your brain light up was off-limits. Still, that was my PET scan
song, and even now the lyrics make me want to lie in a dark room for
an hour and a half while radioactive dye runs through all my veins
and organs. . .

For radiation, I ended up selecting a song that I'd discovered
that summer, when I'd seen the YouTube video "5 Peeps 1 Guitar."
The video was a brilliant cover of Gotye's "Somebody That I Used
to Know," in which the five members of the Canadian band Walk
Off the Earth all squeeze impossibly together, tightly enough to play

---

25. The Episcopal Church, *The Book of Common Prayer and Administration of the
Sacraments and Other Rites and Ceremonies of the Church: Together with the Psalter
or Psalms of David According to the Use of The Episcopal Church* (New York: Church
Publishing, Inc., 1979), 211.

one guitar at the same time. Visually quirky and funny to watch, the hauntingly sad song still sticks to the ribs even after many hearings. I liked to sing the song to my cancer that summer, using the breakup metaphor as a way to wish it goodbye. "Yeah, cancer, you're just somebody that I *used* to know."

When I came in for my first treatment, they told me that in fact I was not allowed to have the phone near me during the treatment. Well, fair enough, I wouldn't want the same stuff they were pouring into my heart to accidentally touch my *phone*, right? They had satellite radio, however, and the pleasant technicians got me positioned on the table under the massive radiation thingies, maneuvered the table just so, swathed my lower half in warm blankets while untying my hospital johnny from the waist up so they could line up my tattoo dots with their scans, and then asked me what I might like to listen to on the radio. Given the usual satellite radio options, I picked the "Coffeehouse" station. I thought acoustic rock would be just the thing to help me relax. The radio came on, and there it was. Not only was the song "Somebody That I Used to Know" playing when they switched on the radio, but it was the Walk Off the Earth cover. Honestly, you can't make this stuff up. What are the odds that of all the songs on the planet that I could have picked, or that might have been playing on any satellite radio station at that moment, it would be a match? Zero. The odds were zero.

That was when I knew I was doing the right thing, and as even more tears of gratitude rolled sideways onto the table, I gave thanks for the gift of that moment. Impossible coincidence, or a sign from above that all would be well? I'll always go with the sign.

EPILOGUE

Falling Stars

Do you remember still the falling stars
that like swift horses through the heavens raced
and suddenly leaped across the hurdles
of our wishes—do you recall? And we
did make so many! For there were countless numbers
of stars: each time we looked above we were
astounded by the swiftness of their daring play,
while in our hearts we felt safe and secure
watching these brilliant bodies disintegrate,
knowing somehow we had survived their fall.

—Rainer Maria Rilke[26]

"We had survived their fall."

When I was a young teen, I heard the news that the war in Vietnam had ended. At that age, all I knew about war endings

---

26. Rainer Maria Rilke, "Falling Stars," in *Rainer Maria Rilke: Selected Poems*, trans. A. E. Flemming (New York: Routledge, [1983] 1990), 210.

was that there were parades, and so I kept looking out of my suburban neighborhood window for days, thinking that a parade might go down our street, and I didn't want to miss it.

Finishing cancer treatment is a little like this. One week you are at the hospital the usual five days in a row, and then you wake up the next week with not a single appointment on your calendar. Treated and released, I was like a stunned trout not sure it can swim away. Would there be a parade? How else would I know it was really over?

As liberating as it is, it is also bizarrely frightening in a way I was not prepared for. I wasn't used to being "un-followed." I had to relearn how to walk around in the world every day without constant reassurance that things were OK. The breach of trust between my brain and the rest of my body is still, three years later, in a process of healing. But in those very first weeks especially, I tiptoed through the world, unsure and shy.

What if it wasn't gone? What if it was coming back fast, and nobody noticed? What if irrevocable damage had been done to my organs and one of them was about to give out? Even the cardiac rehab program I went to at the hospital couldn't reassure me that every time I got my heart rate up, I wouldn't stroke out. Instead of feeling more healthy after treatment, there was a stretch of time where I felt like I was made of glass, and at any moment might break into little pieces, or get hit by a bus.

Furthermore, being so carefully monitored for so many months had been reassuring. Now, in my fragile moments, it felt like I hadn't just broken up with a boyfriend, but with dozens of people who had cared for me, and seen me through these darkest days with compassion and affection. Hello? Didn't anybody care about me anymore?

This reaction stunned me. You think you are going to be dancing the Highland fling all day long, but instead you discover that life is just plodding along, unmoved by your return to its daily ups and downs. My last radiation treatment was on January 3. That morning, after radiation, I had a session with a Reiki practitioner in the radiation department. Then, I went from the hospital to a massage therapist for a full-body massage. The next morning, I had a myofascial release treatment. Then I met with Max. I went to the Athens Diner for lunch to see my peeps there. I had to fill up my own calendar with appointments, just to try to get some equilibrium and reassurance.

Meanwhile, within the following two weeks, I had two intensive, two-day job interviews with parish search teams that flew into town to meet with me. I found myself in the pulpit at my friend Dexter's funeral, having lost him in late December to leukemia. Six weeks after my last treatment, on Valentine's Day, my father passed away peacefully, but unexpectedly, in his sleep. *Whack, whack, whack.* Life continued, but in a way that reminded me that nothing was permanent, that people and things I loved were passing away, even as I continued to live.

The summer after my cancer treatment, I was able to complete the pilgrimage I'd been dreaming of when I got diagnosed, an eight-day retreat at Gampo Abbey on Cape Breton, Nova Scotia. Meditation is still a centerpiece of my life. I moved to the Berkshires of Western Massachusetts to serve a parish there. I've entered the training pathway to become certified to teach Mindfulness-Based Stress Reduction. Slowly I'm beginning to run again, and rebooting my yoga practice. I find living with my body is like living with an adolescent—every day we start from scratch in learning to respect and trust each other. I feel a deep tenderness toward my family, my friends, my parishioners, treasuring the opportunity to share this life with them.

I had thought that this book would have a triumphant ending. I would dearly love to say that I live each day now to the fullest, and that I have learned to maintain a superhuman level of equanimity and mindful detachment, but that would not be my truth.

I emerged from my cancer pilgrimage still human. However, perhaps the one thing I have learned on the journey is that human is good enough for me. I have good days and bad days. Sometimes I remember not to label, and to live in this very moment. Sometimes I "wake up" in a moment and notice how far away I have wandered, or how lost I feel. Sometimes I remember that every minute of every day is a gift, and sometimes I forget and feel frustration or tension at small things that don't really matter.

Of all the lessons, the biggest and hardest for me to practice is self-compassion. All day, every day, I have opportunities not to beat myself up, not to criticize myself or feel frustration at my limits, my failings, and my frailties. At every step of my pilgrimage, I stepped onto and off of this path, and it remains my path to walk.

For you, dear reader, wherever you find yourself today, I wish for you this healing and blessing on your own pilgrimages, and for all the days of your life.

> *May you have happiness, and the causes of happiness.*
> *May you be free from suffering, and the causes of suffering.*
> *May you never be separated from freedom's true joy.*
> —traditional Buddhist prayer

> *Holy God, may we "cast all our care on you who care for us . . . that no clouds of this mortal life may hide from us the light of that love which is immortal."*
> —Book of Common Prayer, p. 216–17